DATE DUE

NOV 23 2007	
MAY 12 2008	

DEMCO, INC. 38-2931

Diego Rivera

Consulting Editors

Hispanics of Achievement

Diego Rivera

James Cockcroft

Chelsea House Publishers
New York Philadelphia

CHELSEA HOUSE PUBLISHERS

Editor-in-Chief: Remmel Nunn
Managing Editor: Karyn Gullen Browne
Copy Chief: Juliann Barbato
Picture Editor: Adrian G. Allen
Art Director: Maria Epes
Deputy Copy Chief: Mark Rifkin
Assistant Art Director: Noreen Romano
Manufacturing Manager: Gerald Levine
Systems Manager: Lindsey Ottman
Production Manager: Joseph Romano
Production Coordinator: Marie Claire Cebrián

Hispanics of Achievement
Senior Editor: John W. Selfridge

Staff for DIEGO RIVERA
Copy Editor: Joseph Roman
Editorial Assistant: Martin Mooney
Picture Researcher: Nisa Rauschenberg
Cover Illustration: Patti Oleon

First Printing

1 3 5 7 9 8 6 4 2

Library of Congress Cataloging-in-Publication Data
Cockcroft, James D.
   Diego Rivera/James D. Cockcroft
      p. cm.—(Hispanics of achievement)
   Includes bibliographical references and index.
   Summary: Examines the life and times of the noted Mexican
muralist, discussing his art and politics.
   ISBN 0-7910-1252-2
         0-7910-1279-4 (pbk.)
   1. Rivera, Diego, 1886–1957. 2. Painters—Mexico—Biography.
[1. Rivera, Diego, 1886–1957. 2. Artists. 3. Painting, Modern—
Mexico. 4. Art appreciation.] I. Title.
ND259.R5C57 1991
759.972—dc20   91-6277
[B]   CIP
[92]   AC

JB
RIVERA

Contents

Hispanics of Achievement

Oscar Arias Sánchez
Costa Rican president

Joan Baez
Mexican-American folksinger

Rubén Blades
Panamanian lawyer and entertainer

Jorge Luis Borges
Argentine writer

Juan Carlos
king of Spain

Pablo Casals
Spanish cellist and conductor

Miguel de Cervantes
Spanish writer

Cesar Chavez
Mexican-American labor leader

El Cid
Spanish military leader

Roberto Clemente
Puerto Rican baseball player

Plácido Domingo
Spanish singer

El Greco
Spanish artist

Gloria Estefan
Cuban-American singer

Gabriel García Márquez
Colombian writer

Raul Julia
Puerto Rican actor

Diego Maradona
Argentine soccer player

José Martí
Cuban revolutionary and poet

Rita Moreno
Puerto Rican singer and actress

Pablo Neruda
Chilean poet and diplomat

Antonia Novello
U.S. surgeon general

Octavio Paz
Mexican poet and critic

Javier Pérez de Cuéllar
Peruvian diplomat

Anthony Quinn
Mexican-American actor

Diego Rivera
Mexican artist

Antonio López de Santa Anna
Mexican general and politician

George Santayana
Spanish poet and philosopher

Junípero Serra
Spanish missionary and explorer

Lee Trevino
Mexican-American golfer

Pancho Villa
Mexican revolutionary

CHELSEA HOUSE PUBLISHERS

INTRODUCTION

Hispanics of Achievement

Rodolfo Cardona

The Spanish language and many other elements of Spanish culture are present in the United States today and have been since the country's earliest beginnings. Some of these elements have come directly from the Iberian Peninsula; others have come indirectly, by way of Mexico, the Caribbean basin, and the countries of Central and South America.

Spanish culture has influenced America in many subtle ways, and consequently many Americans remain relatively unaware of the extent of its impact. The vast majority of them recognize the influence of Spanish culture in America, but they often do not realize the great importance and long history of that influence. This is partly because Americans have tended to judge the Hispanic influence in the United States in statistical terms rather than to look closely at the ways in which individual Hispanics have profoundly affected American culture. For this reason, it is fitting that Americans obtain more than a passing acquaintance with the origins of these Spanish cultural elements and gain an understanding of how they have been woven into the fabric of American society.

It is well documented that Spanish seafarers were the first to explore and colonize many of the early territories of what is today called the United States of America. For this reason, students of geography discover Hispanic names all over the map of the United States. For instance, the Strait of Juan de Fuca was named after the Spanish explorer who first navigated the waters of the Pacific Northwest; the names of states such as Arizona (arid zone), Montana (mountain), Florida (thus named because it was reached on Easter Sunday, which in Spanish is called the feast of Pascua Florida), and California (named after a fictitious land in one of the first and probably the most popular among the Spanish novels of chivalry, *Amadis of Gaul*) are all derived from Spanish; and there are numerous mountains, rivers, canyons, towns, and cities with Spanish names throughout the United States.

Not only explorers but many other illustrious figures in Spanish history have helped define American culture. For example, the 13th-century king of Spain, Alfonso X, also known as the Learned, may be unknown to the majority of Americans, but his work on the codification of Spanish law has greatly influencedthe evolution of American law, particularly in the jurisdictions of the Southwest. For this contribution a statue of him stands in the rotunda of the Capitol in Washington, D.C. Likewise, the name Diego Rivera may be unfamiliar to most Americans, but this Mexican painter influenced many American artists whose paintings, commissioned during the Great Depression and the New Deal era of the 1930s, adorn the walls of government buildings throughout the United States. In recent years the contributions of Puerto Ricans, Mexicans, Mexican Americans (Chicanos), and Cubans in American cities such as Boston, Chicago, Los Angeles, Miami, Minneapolis, New York, and San Antonio have been enormous.

The importance of the Spanish language in this vast cultural complex cannot be overstated. Spanish, after all, is second only to English as the most widely spoken of Western languages within the United States as well as in the entire world. The popularity of the Spanish language in America has a long history.

In addition to Spanish exploration of the New World, the great Spanish literary tradition served as a vehicle for bringing the language and culture to America. Interest in Spanish literature in America began when English immigrants brought with them translations of Spanish masterpieces of the Golden Age. As early as 1683, private libraries in Philadelphia and Boston contained copies of the first picaresque novel, *Lazarillo de Tormes*, translations of Francisco de Quevedo's *Los Sueños*, and copies of the immortal epic of reality and illusion *Don Quixote*, by the great Spanish writer Miguel de Cervantes. It would not be surprising if Cotton Mather, the arch-Puritan, read *Don Quixote* in its original Spanish, if only to enrich his vocabulary in preparation for his writing *La fe del cristiano en 24 artículos de la Institución de Cristo, enviada a los españoles para que abran sus ojos* (The Christian's Faith in 24 Articles of the Institution of Christ, Sent to the Spaniards to Open Their Eyes), published in Boston in 1699.

Over the years, Spanish authors and their works have had a vast influence on American literature—from Washington Irving, John Steinbeck, and Ernest Hemingway in the novel to Henry Wadsworth Longfellow and Archibald MacLeish in poetry. Such important American writers as James Fenimore Cooper, Edgar Allan Poe, Walt Whitman, Mark Twain, and Herman Melville all owe a sizable debt to the Spanish literary tradition. Some writers, such as Willa Cather and Maxwell Anderson, who explored Spanish themes they came into contact with in the American Southwest and Mexico, were influenced less directly but no less profoundly.

Important contributions to a knowledge of Spanish culture in the United States were also made by many lesser known individuals—teachers, publishers, historians, entrepreneurs, and others—with a love for Spanish culture. One of the most significant of these contributions was made by Abiel Smith, a Harvard College graduate of the class of 1764, when he bequeathed stock worth $20,000 to Harvard for the support of a professor of French and Spanish. By 1819 this endowment had produced enough income to appoint a professor, and the philologist and humanist George Ticknor became the first holder of the Abiel Smith Chair, which was the very first endowed Chair at Harvard University. Other illustrious holders of the Smith Chair would include the poets Henry Wadsworth Longfellow and James Russell Lowell.

A highly respected teacher and scholar, Ticknor was also a collector of Spanish books, and as such he made a very special contribution to America's knowledge of Spanish culture. He was instrumental in amassing for Harvard libraries one of the first and most impressive collections of Spanish books in the United States. He also had a valuable personal collection of Spanish books and manuscripts, which he bequeathed to the Boston Public Library.

With the creation of the Abiel Smith Chair, Spanish language and literature courses became part of the curriculum at Harvard, which also went on to become the first American university to offer graduate studies in Romance languages. Other colleges and universities throughout the United States gradually followed Harvard's example, and today Spanish language and culture may be studied at most American institutions of higher learning.

No discussion of the Spanish influence in the United States, however brief, would be complete without a mention of the Spanish influence on art. Important American artists such as John Singer Sargent, James A. M. Whistler, Thomas Eakins, and Mary Cassatt all explored Spanish subjects and experimented with Spanish techniques. Virtually every serious American artist living today has studied the work of the Spanish masters as well as the great 20th-century Spanish painters Salvador Dalí, Joan Miró, and Pablo Picasso.

The most pervasive Spanish influence in America, however, has probably been in music. Compositions such as Leonard Bernstein's *West Side Story*, the Latinization of William Shakespeare's *Romeo and Juliet* set in New York's Puerto Rican quarter, and Aaron Copland's *Salon Mexico* are two obvious examples. In general, one can hear the influence of Latin rhythms—from tango to mambo, from guaracha to salsa—in virtually every form of American music.

This series of biographies, which Chelsea House has published under the general title HISPANICS OF ACHIEVEMENT, constitutes further recognition of—and a renewed effort to bring forth to the consciousness of America's young people—the contributions that Hispanic people have made not only in the United States but throughout the civilized world. The men and women who are featured in this series have attained a high level of accomplishment in their respective fields of endeavor and have made a permanent mark on American society.

The title of this series must be understood in its broadest possible sense: The term *Hispanics* is intended to include Spaniards, Spanish Americans, and individuals from many countries whose language and culture have either direct or indirect Spanish origins. The names of many of the people included in this series will be immediately familiar; others will be less recognizable. All, however, have attained recognition within their own countries, and often their fame has transcended their borders.

The series HISPANICS OF ACHIEVEMENT thus addresses the attainments and struggles of Hispanic people in the United States and seeks to tell the stories of individuals whose personal and professional lives in some way reflect the larger Hispanic experience. These stories are exemplary of what human beings can accomplish, often against daunting odds and by extraordinary personal sacrifice, where there is conviction and determination. Fray Junípero Serra, the 18th-century Spanish Franciscan missionary, is one such individual. Although in very poor health, he devoted the last 15 years of his life to the foundation of missions throughout California—then a mostly unsettled expanse of land— in an effort to bring a better life to Native Americans through the cultivation of crafts and animal husbandry. An example from recent times, the Mexican-American labor leader Cesar Chavez has battled bitter opposition and made untold personal sacrifices in his effort to help poor agricultural workers who have been exploited for decades on farms throughout the Southwest.

The talent with which each one of these men and women may have been endowed required dedication and hard work to develop and become fully realized. Many of them have enjoyed rewards for their efforts during their own lifetime, whereas others have died poor and unrecognized. For some it took a long time to achieve their goals, for others success came at an early age, and for still others the struggle continues. All of them, however, stand out as people whose lives have made a difference, whose achievements we need to recognize today and should continue to honor in the future.

Diego Rivera

Diego Rivera, one of the most brilliant and controversial artists of the 20th century, was born in Guanajuato, Mexico, on December 8, 1886. His murals, the work for which he is best known, depict the plight of laborers and peasants in a world dominated by the wealthy and powerful.

CHAPTER ONE

Only in America

Balanced high on a scaffold in the lobby of the RCA Building in Rockefeller Center, New York City, the renowned Mexican artist Diego Rivera stepped back to assess his work. The excited spectators below, who for hours had waited on line to buy tickets that cold April day in 1933, gasped at the splendor of Rivera's unfinished creation. Janitors, carpenters, and construction workers paused from their labors to gaze up, murmuring to one another and nodding with approval.

Many in the crowd were art students and art lovers who stood in awe of the man critics had hailed as the painter of the first mural masterworks in the 20th century. Others had come because they wanted to catch a glimpse of the outrageous Rivera and his wife, Frida Kahlo, 21 years his junior, who was often seen at the mural site, dressed in long, colorful Mexican wedding costumes and bedecked with pounds of costume jewelry.

A liar or a spinner of tall tales, depending on who was speaking about him, Rivera was noted for his leftist politics. Also, the gossip columnists of the day loved to write about Rivera's wives and lovers.

The onlookers quickly forgot the personal scuttlebutt as they watched Rivera at work. He dipped his paintbrush into a mix of ground colors on a kitchen plate and dabbed deftly at a sketch of a worker's face in the right center of the immense wall. Then he paused again to examine the results, brush poised in midair. An ash from his six-inch cigar protruding from the left side of his mouth fell on a tail of his gray work shirt that draped his ample middle. His froglike eyes seemed to bulge as he worked intently. His hands were remarkably soft, curved, and small for a 6-foot-tall man weighing well over 250 pounds.

A glass of milk and a plate of food left for him by Frida Kahlo lay untouched at Rivera's feet. Although when he started some weeks back he had painted from midafternoon until the early morning hours and then gone out to eat, he now often stayed on the scaffold through the night. He was rushing to meet the May 1 deadline—May Day, the international workers' holiday.

Nelson Rockefeller, the 24-year-old executive vice-president of Rockefeller Center, Inc., director of New York's Museum of Modern Art, and future vice-president of the United States, sat with the artist on the scaffolding some of those nights, watching Rivera work. Rockefeller was the second son of the billionaire John D. Rockefeller, Jr., and Abby Aldrich Rockefeller, a founder of the Museum of Modern Art. The Rockefellers had wined and dined Rivera during his first New York visit in 1931, when his one-man show at the museum had broken all attendance records.

In his inherited role as patron of the arts, Nelson Rockefeller had defended Rivera's controversial 1932 Detroit murals against the protests of angry conservatives and had persuaded the artist to come to New York to paint a mural at Rockefeller Center. Then, as now, it was fashionable for the rich to be seen rubbing shoulders with great artists. The Rockefellers knew about Rivera's earlier murals depicting Nelson Rockefeller's father and grandfather as ugly, greedy robber barons. The Rockefellers were aware of Rivera's socialist beliefs, but secure in their power and wealth, they basked in the prestige of serving as chief American patrons of the man

Rivera works on Man at the Crossroads *at Rockefeller Center's 70-story RCA Building in New York City. The American billionaire Nelson Rockefeller commissioned Rivera to paint the mural in 1933, but he dismissed the artist soon after the painting's leftist imagery began to take form.*

critics had compared to Michelangelo, the great Italian who painted the Sistine Chapel.

Before signing the contract for his huge 1,071-square-foot mural, Rivera had submitted to the Rockefellers a complete sketch and a written description of its explosive composition, including the unspecified face of a labor leader, the face he was about to paint now.

The Rockefellers had offered him the best location, the main lobby of the 70-story RCA Building. Once completed, the 16-building complex, Rockefeller Center, would include several murals, sculptures, landscaped gardens, mosaic tiling, an ice-skating rink, a subway station, offices, radio and television studios, Radio City Music Hall, and the Time-Life Building.

Despite the enormity of the project, Rivera had accepted a small commission of $21,000, payable in installments. Moreover, the fee would have to cover all of his supplies and the salaries of the assistants he needed to undertake the giant fresco mural. Clearly, it was not the money that drew Rivera to New York. He had long proclaimed that art was for people, not something to be displayed in galleries and bought by the wealthy for their private homes. He would be painting, as he wrote 10 months later, for all those inhabitants of the city who would pass through the midtown hub of Rockefeller Center. Thousands would see his mural—not

just the office workers in Rockefeller Center but also the many
unemployed men and women who were lining up for a job on the
huge construction project. Like the rest of the world, America was
in the midst of a severe economic depression, triggered by the
stock market crash of 1929, which had left countless Americans
out of work.

Rivera gazed up at his two-thirds completed creation and felt
a surge of satisfaction. His mural integrated all the themes he had
proposed when he accepted the RCA Building management's
wordy topic: *Man at the Crossroads Looking with Uncertainty but with
Hope and High Vision to the Choosing of a Course Leading to a New and
Better Future.*

"The center of my mural," Rivera wrote in his autobiography,
"showed a worker at the controls of a large machine. . . . Two
elongated ellipses crossed and met in the figure of the worker: one
showing the wonders of the telescope and its revelations of bodies
in space; the other showing the microscope and its discoveries. . . .
Above the germinating soil at the bottom, I projected two visions
of civilization."

No one had objected to Rivera's two sharply contrasting visions.
On the left, he had painted his dark world: society's wealthy elites,
"the debauched rich," drinking, playing cards, and dancing at a
nightclub. Next to them were mounted police clubbing workers
carrying banners, one of which read "We Want Work, Not Charity."
On the right, Rivera painted his bright world. Hunger, oppression,
disorder, and war were eliminated by socialism, the placing of
power in the hands of the people.

When the mural was still a sketch, the face of a workers' leader
had remained undefined. But as Rivera studied his work, an idea
took hold, one that would help make this mural the most
publicized in history. The labor leader in his original sketch, bringing together the figures of a soldier, a black farmer, and a white
worker, would have to be Lenin, the late leader of the world's first

socialist revolution, the Russian Revolution, and the founder of the Soviet Union.

The Rockefellers had not objected to Rivera's scenes of debauched partying capitalists, oppressive police, or socialist athletes and workers. So Rivera had no reason to believe that his sponsors would object to his painting the face of Lenin into the mural. In fact, on one of her frequent visits to the mural site, Abby Aldrich Rockefeller had lavished praise on Rivera for his depiction of May Day demonstrations in the Soviet Union.

Rivera took one final, closer look at the area of the outlined labor leader's face. The day before, he had sketched this area by applying red ocher over the charcoal lines of the third plaster coat. That night, an assistant had traced his design and others had applied a fourth coat of plaster followed by a fifth smoothly polished lime-based intonaco coat. Then they had pounced and stenciled the traced design onto the intonaco.

Now, as his assistants went on grinding colors nearby, the artist deftly brushed in the final details of the area. The technique was second nature to him. He was, after all, the man known for having

The Russian revolutionary Lenin joins hands with workers of diverse nationalities in a panel from Man at the Crossroads. *The Rockefellers, extremely successful capitalists, objected to the depiction of Lenin, a Communist, as a friend of the people and demanded that Rivera alter the panel. The artist refused.*

revitalized fresco wall painting in 1923. He had to work rapidly to finish before the water evaporated. If the lime dried, the paint pigment would bind to the plaster. If his hand slipped, to correct the error he would have to cut away the entire section and prepare the wall all over again.

As Rivera painted, the spectators gasped and murmured. They recognized the dark, alert eyes of Lenin, his high forehead and balding pate, his slightly arched eyebrow, his trimmed mustache, and his narrowing goatee-covered chin. Lenin's hand clasped the three workers' hands that reached out to him.

As word spread about the depiction of Lenin in the mural, there erupted the most turbulent controversy of the artist's already stormy career. "Rivera Perpetrates Scenes of Communist Activity for RCA Walls—and Rockefeller Jr. Foots the Bill" was the headline in New York's *World-Telegram* on April 24, 1933. It was the first shot in what became known as the Battle of Rockefeller Center.

Developments came swiftly. Additional uniformed guards arrived to prevent photographers from entering the RCA Building. Rivera's Swiss-American assistant, Lucienne Bloch, managed to hide behind a curtain and photograph ten close-up shots and one complete view of the mural. Rivera suspected, correctly, that the photos would provide the only lasting record of his magnificent creation.

On May 4, there arrived from Nelson Rockefeller a letter pointing out that potential tenants in the office building would find the image of Lenin offensive. "I am afraid we must ask you to substitute the face of some unknown man," Rockefeller wrote.

Rivera immediately conferred with his assistants. All of them agreed that if Rivera surrendered to Rockefeller's demand, more changes would be requested later. On May 6, the artist answered Rockefeller. Instead of agreeing to remove Lenin's face from the wall, Rivera offered to balance the mural by including the face of a few great Americans, such as Abraham Lincoln.

On May 9, 1933, a dozen guards surrounded Rivera's mural. A representative of Rockefeller Center's managing agents handed

Rivera portrayed his battle with the Rockefellers over the RCA Building mural as an arm-wrestling match with John D. Rockefeller, Sr. Rivera insisted that the rich must not be allowed to dictate the content of art, whereas the Rockefellers were concerned that the leftist political imagery of Rivera's mural would offend their wealthy business associates.

Rivera a check for the unpaid balance of his fee and officially informed him that his commission was canceled. Rivera's assistants raced to a window and scrawled across it "Workers Unite! Help Protect Rivera Mural." Radio City employees quickly covered the mural with tar paper and a preconstructed wooden screen and hung a heavy curtain across the entrance to the lobby. Outside, crowds chanted their support for Rivera. Like a living dramatization of the scene Rivera had painted on the mural, mounted police rushed in swinging their billy clubs.

Rivera and Kahlo's Barbizon Plaza hotel suite was swamped with telegrams expressing support for the artist and his right to creative freedom. But those who objected to the Rockefeller clan's decision had no power to alter it. The power was instead in the hands of America's wealthy "patrons of the arts." The same people who had only days before longed to meet the eccentric artist and his exotic wife quickly united against Rivera. On May 12, 1933, General Motors canceled Rivera's commission for a mural in its building at the 1933 Chicago World's Fair.

Interviewed on the radio, Rivera explained, "Let us take as an example an American millionaire who buys the Sistine Chapel, which contains the work of Michelangelo. . . . Would that millionaire have the right to destroy the Sistine Chapel? . . . In human creation there is something that belongs to humanity at large. . . . No individual owner has the right to destroy it."

With these words, Rivera revealed his fear that the mural would be destroyed. The Rockefellers' pledge was published in the *World-Telegram* on May 12, 1933: "The uncompleted fresco of Diego Rivera will not be destroyed, nor in any way mutilated, but . . . will be covered, to remain hidden for an indefinite time."

Several wealthy individuals offered to pay for the removal and preservation of Rivera's *Man at the Crossroads.* Nelson Rockefeller announced that he was exploring the possibility of transferring the mural to the Museum of Modern Art. Ten months later, the unthinkable happened. On the weekend of February 10–11, 1934, Rivera's entire mural was ripped off the wall and smashed to bits.

At his home in Mexico City, Rivera heard the terrible news. He dashed off a cable published by New York's *Herald Tribune*, accusing the Rockefellers of "an act of cultural vandalism."

There was no response from the Rockefellers for an amazing 33 years.

Rivera's refusal to alter Man at the Crossroads *to suit the Rockefellers prompted Nelson Rockefeller to dismiss the artist, cover the panels, and station policemen in the building's lobby. The controversy surrounding the project resulted in the destruction of the mural by the Rockefellers in a gross act of censorship.*

In the aftermath of the controversy, Rivera painted a smaller version of Man at the Crossroads. *In this detail of the reconstructed version, workers gather around the Russian revolutionary Leon Trotsky (wearing glasses) and the German philosopher and economist Karl Marx (bearded, far right).*

Rivera was long dead when Nelson Rockefeller presented his version of the controversy in an April 1967 article for the *New York Times Magazine.* He blamed Frida Kahlo for having influenced her husband to add "unbelievable" political images. "Whenever I went out Frida came in," complained Rockefeller. "Then he had Stalin—or was it Lenin? I've forgotten—featured in the center of the mural." Rockefeller concluded: "Then we gave him his final check and thanked him, and just took the mural down." Rockefeller knew that Rivera's gigantic fresco mural was not "just taken down" but had been destroyed in a violent and blatant act of censorship.

Rivera had always seemed to relish the limelight of scandal and conflict. But he was devastated by the destruction of his Rockefeller Center mural. In 1934, at Mexico City's Palace of Fine Arts, he produced a smaller version of *Man at the Crossroads,* to "bring the murdered painting back to life." He made a few changes, including the addition of the figure of John D. Rockefeller, Jr., in the nightclub scene. The painting of the smaller version of the mural was sweet revenge for Rivera, but it could not compensate for the rape of its prototype, the mural at Rockefeller Center. Only in America, he said, could wealthy men be permitted to commit such callous acts.

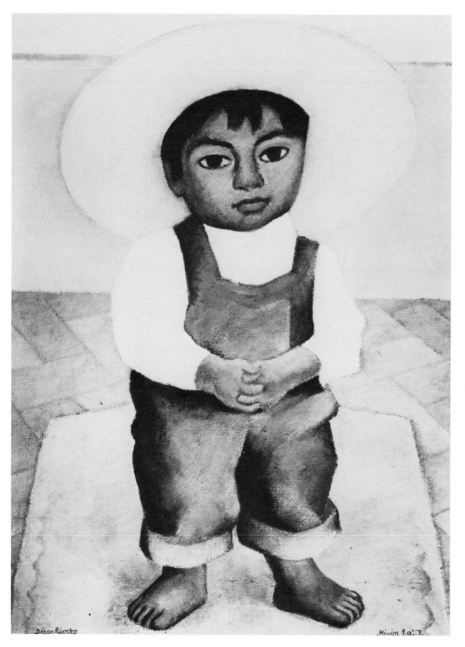

Not all of Rivera's work depicted grand spectacles of political struggle; he was also a master portraitist, inspired by the simple, colorful images of his native culture. Rivera painted this sensitive portrait of a young boy in 1927.

CHAPTER TWO

The Wonder Child

Diego Rivera was born on December 8, 1886, in a modest house at 80 Pocitos Street in the center of Guanajuato, a picturesque old mining city in the Sierra Madres, 170 miles northwest of Mexico City. Guanajuato's people were among the first to participate in Mexico's Wars of Independence against Spain (1810–21). They broke into the city's granaries, liberated several surrounding towns, and almost seized Mexico City. Someday Rivera would depict their heroics in his murals.

But on that day in 1886, fear hovered over the Rivera household when María del Pilar Barrientos de Rivera, a petite 26-year-old woman, informed her husband that her labor pains had started. It was her fourth pregnancy in the four years they were married. Three times the young woman had given birth to lifeless babies. Her husband, Diego Rivera, a black-bearded mountain of a man, 12 years her senior, was nearby, gently consoling her.

María's older unmarried sister, Cesaria del Pilar Barrientos, ran off to alert the doctor. Then she dashed to the church of Nuestra Señora de Guanajuato to pray that her sister would bear a live child.

Within hours, Cesaria and her brother-in-law broke into smiles and tears of joy when they heard an infant's cry instead of the usual sound of María weeping. The doctor emerged from the bedroom and held up two fingers. Twins!

Eleven days later, the births were recorded in the civil register, Diego María Rivera and Carlos María Rivera, their middle names reflecting their mother's gratitude to the Virgin Mary. When she was stronger, María Rivera, accompanied by her sister, her unmarried great aunt, Vicenta, and the children's nurse, Antonia, took the babies to be baptized. Diego's baptismal name was Diego María de la Concepción Juan Nepomuceno Estanislao de la Rivera y Barrientos Acosta y Rodríguez.

Rivera's ancestors were of modest means. His paternal grandfather, Anastasio Rivera, was born in Spain and migrated to Mexico, where he purchased a small silver mine. At the age of 50, he married a 17-year-old girl, Ynez Acosta, a Mexican of Portuguese-Jewish descent. In the 1860s, he joined Benito Juárez's army of national liberation in the war against the French. He died of mysterious causes, leaving his young widow debt ridden. She raised their nine children alone. One of them, Diego's father, worked

Perhaps more than any other individual, the Mexican revolutionary Benito Juárez shaped the history of modern Mexico. Born to Zapotec parents in Oaxaca, Mexico, in 1806, he rose from poverty to become a lawyer and served as president of Mexico during the 1860s and 1870s.

Rivera painted Open Air School *in 1934. A man of strong political beliefs, Rivera's father was committed to education as a means of improving the lot of the impoverished Mexican Indians. For a time he served as a rural school inspector and visited schools such as the one in this painting.*

hard and became a grade school teacher. Diego's mother was also raised in a fatherless home. Her mother, Nemesia Rodríguez de Barrientos, of mixed Spanish and Indian ancestry, supported her two daughters, María and Cesaria, by running a small sweetshop.

Determined to turn things around for his family, Diego's father bought an interest in a mine with borrowed money, was elected a city councilor, and received a state appointment as a rural school inspector. He believed that the poverty of Mexico's rural Indians could be overcome through education. He hoped to rise to a more important political office and be in a position to act on his dreams of social reform. He also thought about starting a newspaper.

During this period in Mexico, government power was being consolidated by a Liberal, Porfirio Díaz, a part-Indian general who had defeated the French in the Battle of Puebla on May 5, 1862. At last the anticlerical Liberals had overcome the Conservatives—the political voice of the Catholic church (Mexico's largest landholding and banking institution until the 1850s). For generations, family farmers, rural day laborers, artisans, workers, street vendors, and beggars had served as mere cannon fodder in the warring armies, dragooned by the leading Conservative and Liberal families of wealth. This shameful strife had prostrated

Porfirio Díaz, a part-Indian general who defeated the French in the Battle of Puebla on May 5, 1862, ruled Mexico with an iron hand, repeatedly calling on his army and special police force to quell dissent. When Rivera was 16 years old, he was expelled from school for taking part in anti-Díaz demonstrations.

Mexico, leaving it ripe for foreign takeover, first by the Americans and then the French. From 1846 to 1848, half of Mexico's territory was seized by U.S. soldiers. One of them, Ulysses S. Grant, later the commanding general of the North in the U.S. Civil War, called it "one of the most unjust [wars] ever waged by a stronger against a weaker nation." Congressman Abraham Lincoln, later to be U.S. president during the Civil War, concurred.

After the Liberals finally gained control of a weakened Mexican government and promulgated the anticlerical 1857 Constitution, the Conservatives invited in the French, who set up Archduke Maximilian and his wife, Carlota of Austria, as emperor and empress.

Led by a full-blooded Zapotec Indian lawyer named Benito Juárez (called the Abraham Lincoln of Mexico), the Liberals' guerrilla fighters repeatedly cut down the French Foreign Legion's search-and-destroy missions in the provinces. Some 50,000 Mexicans died in the victorious war of national liberation.

In 1867, European leaders implored Juárez to rescind his order to execute the emperor and empress. Juárez replied that it was the emperor who had decreed the death penalty for prisoners and so was only receiving his own brand of justice. Later, Rivera would paint into his murals a stern, dark Indian (Juárez) facing a tall blond Nordic (Maximilian), the tips of guerrilla rifles spitting fire at the emperor's head: a symbol of Indo-America's revenge on imperialistic Europe.

Now with General Díaz in power, the senior Diego thought that perhaps Mexico would move toward prosperity. But bad luck quickly plagued both the Rivera family and their nation.

When the twins were less than two years old, Carlos fell ill and died. María Rivera plunged into a deep depression. She stayed near Carlos's tomb and refused to go home, neglecting her son Diego. Her family called a doctor friend, who urged her to study for a career in obstetrics. Finally, she heeded his advice and registered in school, leaving little Diego in the care of his Indian nurse, a woman he recalled loving "more than my mother."

Diego was an exceptionally bright and observant child who showed early signs of artistic inclination. By the time he was four, he was grabbing whatever pens and pencils he could find around the house and drawing on everything—furniture, walls, loose papers. To stop the defacement, his father covered the walls of a room with canvas and presented his son with a box of crayons and pencils. Diego now had his very first studio.

Dieguito, as his family called him, liked to play with trains and other mechanical objects, taking them apart to see how they worked and then drawing them on the walls—"my first murals" he later called them. His fascination with rail and mining machinery earned him the nickname the Engineer by age six. He spent hours at Guanajuato's railroad depot. One of his earliest drawings, made when he was only two or three, was of a locomotive with a caboose, moving steadily uphill.

Rivera's inquisitive and argumentative nature surfaced early. His great-aunt Vicenta, called Totota by the family, believed that her nephew sorely needed religious training to curb his rebellious nature. She took him to the shrine of the Virgin Mary in the same church where his aunt Cesaria had prayed for his safe birth and instructed him to pray that his mother would pass her diploma exams, scheduled for the next day.

Her little nephew dared to refuse, shouting at his aunt that the saint was made of wood and obviously could not hear their prayers. The next day, when his mother passed her exams despite his refusal to pray, Dieguito instantly became a nonbeliever. Many of the townspeople shunned the youngest atheist in Guanajuato, but the anticlerical friends of his father were elated and called him their younger brother.

An economic depression in 1892 hit Guanajuato hard. The silver mine owned by Diego's father was one of many that failed, and his dream of a new Mexico under Díaz suddenly seemed no more than a wild fantasy. Díaz's tyrannical 35-year rule, from 1876 to 1911, became known as the Porfiriato. His slogan was "Effective Suffrage, No Reelection," but after 1884 he had himself regularly reelected. Diego's father resented both Díaz's rapprochement with the Catholic church and his selling of the nation's resources to foreigners. Díaz's army and a special rural police force, the Rurales, crushed any hint of popular protest.

Diego's father had started a weekly newspaper, *El Democrata*, exhorting Liberals to concern themselves with the living conditions of the poor. But during hard times, charity and generosity were not popular notions. The newspaper's columns, combined with Dieguito's outrageous behavior in church, incurred the wrath of the town.

The Rivera family moved to Mexico City, where Diego Sr. hoped to find a manufacturing job or perhaps a position in the rapidly expanding bureaucracy of the Díaz dictatorship. But the Cientificos, or Scientific Ones, as the tight little clique surrounding Díaz called themselves, were not inclined to favor outsiders. They envisioned the construction of a modern capitalist Mexico where they would be the first to prosper. The end result of their policies was the delivery of Mexico's lands, factories, oil fields, mines, railroads, and work force to U.S. and European owners. Rural Mexico resembled a giant plantation, its peasants virtual slaves on land they had once owned.

In the capital, Dieguito became unhappy and ill, first with scarlet fever and then typhoid. In the cramped house where the family settled, there was no room for his studio. Diego's father was forced to accept a petty desk job in the Department of Health. His mother's midwife practice had to be rebuilt from scratch. Pregnant once more, she gave birth to another son, who lived only a week. For a year, longing for Guanajuato, Dieguito stopped drawing.

In 1894, Diego told his parents he wanted to go to school. His mother insisted on a church school, and soon Diego skipped to the sixth grade. However, when Diego's father stumbled on his son's battle drawings, he decided the boy should follow a military career. He enrolled Diego in a military prep school, but Diego hated the military and quit after one miserable week.

Aunt Totota, concerned as ever to save the rebellious boy's soul, saw her chance when he asked to reexamine her collection of hand-wrought silver jewelry, ceramic sculptures, and miniature carvings. There was more to be seen in the churches, she assured him, and he agreed to accompany her. The church interiors gleamed with elaborate altar pieces of carved, gilded wood, or *retablos*, that served as backdrops for small polychromed statues and oil paintings on pieces of hammered tin, or ex-votos.

Diego stared in awe. But it was not religious fervor that ignited the boy's passions. Rather, it was an instant love for Mexican folk art. He called his own first mural of 1922 "nothing more than a big ex-voto."

At 10, Rivera announced to his startled family that he intended to be an artist. Neither of Diego's parents approved of this decision, understanding that the life of an artist is usually a difficult and uncertain one. But Diego's stubbornness prevailed. His mother enrolled him in a night class at the famous Academy of San Carlos.

At the end of 1898, the oversized 12-year-old graduated from high school with honors. At the academy he won second prize in drawing. He was now eligible to enter the National Preparatory School, where he could prepare for a profession, but again he insisted that art was his only interest. A scholarship of about 15 dollars a month at the academy allowed him to become a day student there at the age of 13.

Rivera was influenced mainly by two artistic traditions—classical European and Mexican folk. At San Carlos, Diego had to follow strict rules of tried-and-true European methods of painting. He hated the academy's emphasis on photographic realism, but he performed with competence, copying from plaster casts and engravings and improving his technique. He learned the laws of perspective and how to create an illusion of depth. One teacher encouraged his love of motion and of the inner workings of things.

Years younger than his fellow students, Rivera came to school in short pants and colored socks. In his pockets he stashed hooks and worms. Only two blocks away was an Indian slum, where the streets intersected with sewage-polluted canals. Sometimes Rivera sneaked out to fish on the banks of these canals. There he would watch as canoes, paddled by Indian men in white pants, moved quietly along the water. Usually with the men were women in embroidered blouses. They hoped their boxes of produce and colorful flowers would bring a good price at the downtown markets. It was a huge festival for young Rivera's artistic imagination. It was on those streets that Rivera met José Guadalupe Posada—the man he later called his most important teacher, the one who taught him that "the soul of every masterpiece is powerful emotion." It would take Rivera years to realize the importance of that lesson.

Every time Rivera passed Posada's small engraving shop, he stopped to stare at its window display. Posada's engravings were made on metal plates, mounted on wooden blocks with letters superimposed to form the words of prayers, jokes, and songs, and then printed on an ancient press. Posada died in 1913 at the age of 61, having engraved more than 15,000 plates. Roving singers and poets bought the colored tissue paper printings and performed musical renditions of Posada's stories. All over the country, illiterate Mexicans—85 percent of the population—bought

Posada's illustrated broadsheets and asked the town reader to help them memorize the words.

Posada's work also filled the pages of the anti-Díaz underground press. At that time, illegal newspapers and student and worker strikes were becoming a major way of fighting for democracy. Fewer people read Liberal papers like Diego's father's *El Democrata*, turning instead to the more radical, irregularly printed underground press. These news sheets were influenced by many varieties of anticapitalist ideas. They had inflammatory names, such as *The Strike*, *The Revolution*, *The Commune*, *The Socialist*, and—the most widely read of all—*Regeneración*, founded in 1900. Similar papers were beginning to appear in the United States, where *Regeneración* had a broad readership among Mexican Americans.

As Diego gawked in at Posada's window, the figures enchanted him. They seemed to be suspended in action, almost alive, nothing like the inanimate figures he dutifully drew at the Academy of San Carlos. Posada could not help but notice the fat young man staring enraptured through his window. The lad's forehead was too high, his eyes too bulged. Posada invited him into his shop, and soon Rivera became a permanent fixture there, watching the older man work. Fascinated by the engraver's unsparing caricatures of Díaz and the rich, Diego absorbed both Posada's art and his revolutionary politics. Decades later, when Rivera was world famous, he painted Posada's likeness on the walls of the National Palace and Hotel del Prado and, along with other artists, reproduced Posada's work.

In 1903, 17-year-old Rivera lost all patience with the Academy of San Carlos. He joined a student strike against Díaz and was among several who were expelled. When the expelled students were reinstated, Diego did not return. He had a need to paint on his own, without restrictions.

He roamed the city and countryside, drawing and painting, choosing his own colors and subjects. Before long he had an overstuffed portfolio of his work.

Rivera's History of Mexico *adorns the National Palace in Mexico City.
The mural caricatures the hated Spanish conquistador Hernán Cortés,
who led a 16th-century expedition to Mexico and directed a bloody
massacre against the Aztec, who tried to stand in the way of his conquests.*

CHAPTER THREE

Mexican Cowboy Abroad

Although his paintings sold well and older artists encouraged him, Rivera was dissatisfied. He switched from oils to pastels, stopped painting to pursue a music hall performer, drank too much, audited an anatomy class at a medical school, and then resumed painting with a frenzied passion. Around this time, he imagined that he was going blind—the beginning of a lifetime of hypochondria.

As the 20th century began, Europe was the mecca for aspiring artists. Rivera, like many other young painters of the day, dreamed of going to Spain, France, and Italy, where the works of the great masters hung in museums and where one could study with the world's greatest teachers.

Diego Rivera's father had become a health inspector for the government, but he could not afford to support a son living abroad. Anxious, as always, to help his only son, he carried a folder of Diego's work with him on a field trip to the Atlantic coastal city of Veracruz. There he showed Governor Teodoro Dehesa some of Diego's drawings. Enormously impressed, Dehesa offered the young artist a monthly stipend from the Veracruz state treasury for art studies in Europe. The only condition was that he send a painting every six months to Dehesa to demonstrate his progress.

The year was 1906, and 20-year-old Diego Rivera bent to the task of earning his transatlantic passage. He exhibited his work at two group shows and with the money from sales raced to purchase a steamship ticket, arriving in Spain on January 6, 1907.

Rivera began his European studies with the successful realist painter Eduardo Chicharro y Aguera. In Spain's art world, the glorious days of El Greco and Goya no longer existed. Spanish art had become a poor imitation of the French. For this reason, young Spanish artists who could scrape up the money left for Paris.

For a year, Rivera studied the masterpieces of Goya, El Greco, Brueghel, and Bosch at Madrid's famous Prado Museum. He copied them, getting the feel of their lines and styles. At night he roamed the cafés, noticed by everyone when he walked in a door— 300 pounds, a broad-brimmed hat, curly beard and unforgettable features, his clothes wrinkled and paint stained, too tight to fit his bulk. Because of his sombrero, he was called the Mexican Cowboy.

Rivera was at ease with strangers and was regarded as a fine addition to café life. Intelligent and charming, he often told jokes and stories to the café patrons. Despite his homely face and huge body, women flocked around the Mexican Cowboy. Avant-garde writers and painters befriended him as well.

Rivera sent the promised samples to Governor Dehesa. A note from Chicharro described his work as magnificent and Rivera as a tireless worker. Governor Dehesa was pleased that he had "adopted" a worthy artist, and Rivera's reputation soon spread in Mexico. Only Rivera was unhappy, later claiming, "I did very little painting of any worth during my year and a half in Spain." After finishing each new canvas, he would go into a rage and run off to a café to stuff himself with food in an effort to relieve his frustration.

As his bulk increased, he embarked on one of many punishing diets, living on nothing but fruits and vegetables, exhausting himself with work, and then indulging in one-night stands with models and women who frequented the cafés. He became ill with skin and glandular disorders, some real and some imaginary. Sometimes his outbursts of rage drove his friends away.

In those days, King Alfonso XIII maintained a tenuous hold over Spain, while the people yearned for a republic. When Alfonso sent army troops to massacre the striking workers of Barcelona and ordered executions of labor leaders, the artists in the cafés talked about little else.

For the first time, Rivera read prodigiously—anarchists, philosophers, the Russian novelists, and then he found the works of Karl Marx. The conflicting ideas confused him, but a shadowy understanding of the world and a hunger to know more had developed in Rivera.

By 1909, Rivera was consumed with restlessness. He took a train to Paris and stayed at a low-priced hotel in the Latin Quarter. He painted in the free academies of Montparnasse and in the open air along the banks of the Seine, frequenting the Paris cafés at night. Rivera and his friends saw the works of the newer painters there. He was impressed by the paintings of Pablo Picasso, a Spaniard living in Paris, but the work of Paul Cézanne especially moved him.

He continued to lack confidence in his own painting. In the summer he wandered with other painters through Spain, Portugal, France, Holland, Belgium, and England—looking for something he could not name. In Brussels, Belgium, he visited museums, staring at the lively crowd scenes of Brueghel and the color and humor of Goya's portraits. He began painting again.

While in Brussels, Rivera met María Gutierrez Blanchard, a woman he knew from his days in Spain. Half Spanish and half French, she was a hunchback but had a lovely face with glowing dark eyes. He also met her Russian friend Angeline Beloff, a young Russian artist, slim and fair haired. "A kind, sensitive, almost unbelievably decent person," Rivera commented later. The three of them went to London.

There, Rivera and Beloff fell in love as they visited museums and walked the streets in what seemed to be a city of poor people. Rivera saw modern industrial slums with their huge factories and witnessed intense poverty. The streets stimulated his study of Karl Marx's analysis of capitalism, the private ownership of a nation's wealth, and the profit motive. This time the ideas seemed clearer. Marx had analyzed this very city and had noticed the same striking contrast between rich and poor.

One day in the British Museum, Rivera came across a collection of preconquest Mexican art, and he "suddenly felt an overmastering need to see my land and my people." Upon his return to Paris, he wrote to Governor Dehesa, requesting permission to come to Mexico for the 1910 centennial celebration of Mexico's independence. He was told to bring his paintings with him for inclusion in an art exhibit at his old school, the Academy of San Carlos. Typical of the Díaz government's love of all things European, most of the space and money was assigned to contemporary works from Spain.

Rivera spent the summer of 1910 in the French countryside, working on new paintings. After a tearful farewell with Angeline Beloff, the two lovers tentatively decided to live together when he returned.

Rivera arrived in Veracruz, Mexico, on October 2 and boarded a train bound for the capital. As he looked out the window, he marveled at the emerald and gold colors of the coastal tropics and, hours later, at the glistening snowcaps of the volcanic mountains between Puebla and Mexico City. He vaguely sensed that it was important for him to draw upon Mexico's natural beauty and Indian costuming in his work.

The centennial art exhibit was scheduled to open on November 20, 1910. This was the same day Francisco Indalecio Madero, a Berkeley-educated friend of Díaz's, had designated for a nationwide uprising to overthrow the dictator. Later, it would become a national holiday. Some rebels began the attack a few days before November 20, and so the art exhibit opened in a tense atmosphere. All but 2 of Rivera's 40 paintings sold that day—several to Díaz's wife and to the Academy of San Carlos.

While high society was flocking to the art show, battle-seasoned regulars of the Mexican Liberal party (PLM), who had launched armed rebellions in 1906 and 1908, were carrying out a full-scale offensive against Díaz. In the following months, they captured town after town in Mexico's northern states. At one point, they overtook the state of Baja California and ran it according to their anarchist philosophy—communal property and self-government. Other anti-Díaz leaders came forward. In the north, the big strapping "cowboy" Francisco "Pancho" Villa and the former chick-pea exporter Álvaro Obregón were among the most prominent. In the south, a somber dark-eyed peasant who had lost his land, Emiliano Zapata, commanded a wide following.

Rivera designed a poster that was mass-produced for Mexican peasants. Underneath a picture of a family plowing its field behind a team of oxen, with Christ fondly gazing on them from the sky, the poster read, The Distribution of Land to the Poor Is Not Contrary to the Teachings of Our Lord Jesus Christ and the Holy Mother Church.

The Mexican general Álvaro Obregón (in light uniform) was a leading figure in the Mexican Revolution. He served as minister of war and, in 1920, became president of Mexico. He was assassinated on July 17, 1928, just before beginning a second term.

It was Rivera's only sketch during this period that expressed his revolutionary ardor. When he saw his paintings collected together in one place at the centennial show, his dissatisfaction with his own work was heightened. He was determined to return to Paris for further study. Also, he had not forgotten Angeline.

But first he went to Morelos. There, Zapata's peasant guerrillas, shouting the old PLM slogan "Land and Liberty," were taking back their lands and setting up what became known as the Morelos Communes—self-sufficient communities of farmers and workers. For the next eight years they would run the world's second-largest area of sugar production without any need for millionaire bosses. During his brief stay, Rivera grew so excited that he forgot even to sketch—but what he saw remained forever etched in his mind.

The charismatic Mexican revolutionary Emiliano Zapata, depicted in this portrait by Rivera, was dedicated to the cause of Mexican liberation through land reform. A skilled horseman and brave military leader, Zapata was killed in an ambush on April 10, 1919.

The Mexican artist José Orozco had his first exhibit in 1915 and became one of the leading figures in Mexico's mural renaissance of the 1920s. Today his work may be seen in the United States—at Dartmouth College, for example—or adorning the walls of buildings such as Mexico City's Ministry of Justice.

Rivera returned to Paris in June 1911 and immediately ran to embrace Angeline Beloff. "Our reunion was rapturous," he said later. "We now decided to live together."

Ironically, while Rivera and Beloff were setting up house, students at the Academy of San Carlos were striking. Blocked by police from entering their school, the students began conducting open-air art classes in the streets. One of them was a 13-year-old youth Rivera would not meet until 1919, David Alfaro Siqueiros. An upper-class lad of Portuguese-Mexican descent, Siqueiros played a minor role in the strike. With Orozco and Rivera, Siqueiros would be the third member of the trio of Mexican muralists called the Big Three who, during Mexico's mural renaissance of the 1920s, would change the art world forever.

In 1911 and 1912, Rivera began receiving money from a grant awarded him by the newly elected Madero government. But he also received depressing news. Madero persuaded Zapata's guerrillas to hand over their weapons, only to have the army general in charge then order his troops to open fire on the disarmed peasants. Mexico's old elites were reestablishing their control, now joined by a new group of self-serving middle-class bureaucrats. The peasant-worker revolution was being betrayed. Despondent and troubled, Rivera plunged back into his artwork.

After spending two years in Spain, Rivera settled in Paris, where he was introduced to the bohemian café life-style of the Montparnasse district. In France, he was influenced by the Spanish painter Pablo Picasso and began experimenting with cubism, an abstract form of art that depicts its subjects as fragmented objects in space.

CHAPTER FOUR

The Artist's Life in Paris

In Paris, Rivera and Angeline Beloff lived in the section of the city called Montparnasse. To a visitor Montparnasse seemed a bohemian paradise. People from all over the world wandered the district's hilly, winding streets and congregated in its cafés. Often intoxicated with drink and drugs, they would laugh and flirt away the nights, joking, telling stories, and carousing until dawn. They considered themselves rebels, and they wore strange costumes and indulged in unconventional behavior to prove it. They had little money and lived from day to day, spending their meager resources without a care.

Rivera's favorite hangout was the Café Rotonde. There, he became close with the young Italian painter and sculptor Amedeo Modigliani. Years Later, Modigliani's delicately wrought oil paintings—nudes with elongated faces and necks—would be worth millions, but when Rivera met him, Modigliani was a poor alcoholic and drug addict.

In 1911, Rivera and Modigliani met frequently at the Rotonde, scandalizing people with their bawdy humor and outrageous yarns and arguing art theory late into the night. Everyone sought out Rivera in his studio or at the café. He was the uncontested champion storyteller and debater of the Rotonde. During the day, Rivera remained in his studio, working himself into a state of exhaustion. Dissatisfied as ever, he swung rapidly from one painting style to another, passionately defending whatever style he was enamored with at the time, only to denounce it later.

Beloff, born in Saint Petersburg, Russia, had studied art and, also like Rivera, was politically active during her youth. After her parents died, she went to Paris. Beloff introduced Rivera to her friends from eastern Europe, and he learned enough Russian to talk with them in the cafés of Montparnasse.

Six years older than Rivera, even-tempered, calm, and maternal, Beloff was perhaps an unlikely match for the unpredictable, self-centered Mexican. Rivera often moped around the studio or burst into temper tantrums that caused visitors to flee in terror. He claimed to be "wrestling with spirits" and often stayed out drinking until dawn.

In the spring of 1912, Rivera and Beloff traveled to Toledo, Spain, a city that reminded him of his beloved childhood home of Guanajuato. Beloff had begun to study Spanish, realizing that someday her exiled lover would yearn for home. Rivera, still searching for his own artistic identity, studied the works of the great Spanish master El Greco for several months.

Cubism was the avant-garde art form then making the biggest splash in European art circles. Picasso had introduced it in Paris in 1907, citing Cézanne's dictum, "You must see in nature the cylinder, the sphere, and the cone." In 1908, Picasso met Georges Braque, and they worked together to take cubism further. Painting with somber grays and tans, the cubists broke down subjects into their component parts and underlying geometric forms. Finally, in analytic cubism, as Picasso called it, there remained only traces of the original subjects, shown from many viewpoints.

In 1913, Rivera's *Girl with Artichokes* marked the start of his journey into cubism. It was his first attempt to portray several

One example of Rivera's cubist work is Sailor, *which he painted in 1914. Though Rivera, like most artists in Paris during the early part of the 20th century, was fascinated by cubism at first, he soon grew disenchanted. By 1918 he was again in search of a form of expression that was uniquely his.*

different views of a figure on one canvas. A late arrival to the cubist scene, Rivera embarked on a punishing schedule for the next four years, producing more than 200 paintings and becoming one of cubism's most prodigious innovators.

But Rivera's own estimate of his cubist years revealed his dissatisfaction. "When it dawned on me that all this innovation had little to do with real life, I would surrender all the glory and acclaim cubism had brought me for a way in art truer to my inmost feelings."

After the assassination of President Madero in 1913, Rivera's source of Mexican funding was cut off. While Beloff painted and sold reproductions of European masterworks to pay the rent, Rivera plunged into the current art rage of the period. During this time, he and Picasso became close friends. Picasso's favorable opinion of Rivera's paintings opened the doors for Rivera's first one-man show, at Paris's Galerie Weill in April 1914.

Rivera worked as if pursued by demons. He had always been excited by the inner workings of objects, by the fields of mechanics and geometry, and cubism focused entirely on those things. He completed at least five paintings a month for Parisian cubist art dealer Leonce Rosenberg, who paid artists according to the size of the painted canvas.

While the cubists painted for a pittance, the governments and private capitalists of the industrialized countries were competing over larger stakes—boundaries, colonies, and spheres of influence, all sources of great wealth. Seeking diamonds, gold, and rubber in Africa, coal in the French province of Alsace-Lorraine, oil in Saudi Arabia, Venezuela, and Mexico, greedy politicians and magnates were rapidly leading their nations toward World War I. When Rivera predicted that war would come to Europe, his friends laughed at what they believed was a very unlikely and overly dismal prophecy.

After Rivera's successful one-man show, he and Beloff, along with their old friend María Gutierrez Blanchard and several others, embarked on a walking and sketching tour of Spain. While they were on the Mediterranean island of Majorca, off the coast of Barcelona, they heard that Archduke Francis Ferdinand of Austria had been assassinated on June 28, 1914. The killing provided a pretext for a four-year global conflict that would cost millions of lives—World War I.

Rivera and his entourage took a ferry to Barcelona and discovered that Russia had declared war on Austria. They joined a workers' street demonstration against the war and returned to Majorca, remaining there for three months. Rivera painted the island's scenery. He developed his own bold cubist style, dipping his brush into bright tropical colors instead of the grays of the other cubists, creating what became known as decorative or synthetic cubism.

Some of Rivera's traveling companions were reserve officers in the French army. They received orders to return home for active duty. With those who remained behind, Rivera and Beloff moved to Barcelona. They had run out of funds and had no way of returning to Paris. Beloff's stipend from Saint Petersburg had run out, too, and she painted the Russian national emblem on the wall of the Russian consulate in Barcelona to earn a little money.

They spent the winter in Madrid. Rivera painted a portrait of a Spanish writer, Ramón Gómez de la Serna, and in early 1915, Gómez de la Serna financed a show of several refugee cubist artists called *Los Integros*, or those with integrity. Madrid's traditionalist art lovers gathered in front of the gallery to sneer at Rivera's unusual portrait of Gómez de la Serna. Fearing a riot would break out, the mayor closed the gallery.

Having difficulty selling his cubist paintings in Spain, Rivera returned to Paris in the spring of 1915. He found Montparnasse almost deserted. A curfew sent everyone scurrying back to their quarters by 10:30 P.M. The city was blacked out against possible German air raids. Prices were sky-high, and there were shortages of heating fuel and foodstuffs.

Beloff and Rivera moved into a cold one-room studio. Because of the war, there were almost no art shows where paintings could be sold. Most of the time the couple existed on thin soups until one of Rivera's paintings or Beloff's reproductions was sold on the street. Then they gorged themselves on meat and cheese, sharing with their equally poverty stricken friends.

For three years, the war was stalemated, with the Germans unable to break through to Paris. Waves of soldiers died in trenches and were then replaced with hundreds of thousands of others. In the first Battle of the Marne, each side suffered half a million casualties. At the Battle of Verdun, half a million more young British and French soldiers were killed. In England and France no one heard about the extent of the slaughter. Rivera and his friends predicted mutiny in the armies, an international revolution when young soldiers, tired of fighting for wealth that they would never share, would turn against their officers.

Rivera began to think about home. He was intrigued by reports that Zapata and Villa had occupied Mexico City. He painted a modified cubist *Zapatista Landscape*, featuring a Mexican sombrero over a wooden box behind a rifle. Throughout 1915 and much of 1916, Rivera experimented with new techniques. He tried wax instead of oil and plaster stucco for a rougher texture. His work gradually became more abstract.

While Rivera was working, Beloff was alone. She told Rivera that she wanted to have a child, but Rivera refused, wanting nothing to interfere with his work. But Beloff got her way. On August 11, 1916, she gave birth to a son, Diego, Jr.

Better off after some successful New York exhibitions and sales, Rivera and Beloff moved to a larger apartment. Still, life in wartime

(continued on page 57)

A portrait of Angeline Beloff painted by Rivera. The artistic and intensely political Beloff seemed a good match for Rivera, and the two fell in love soon after their first meeting. But Rivera's unpredictable moods and often violent temper tantrums made their relationship a difficult one.

The Paintings of
Diego Rivera

Calle de Pueblo (1909), oil on canvas.

Nature Morte au Cigare (1916), oil on canvas.

Workers' Meeting (1923–24), fresco, Ministry of Education mural.

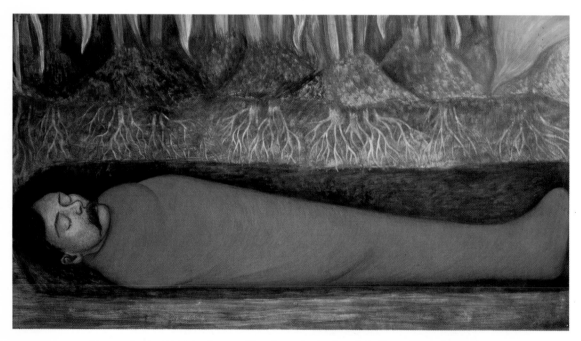

Zapata Buried (1926), fresco, Chapingo Agricultural College Chapel mural.

History of Mexico (1928), fresco, Mexico City National Palace mural.

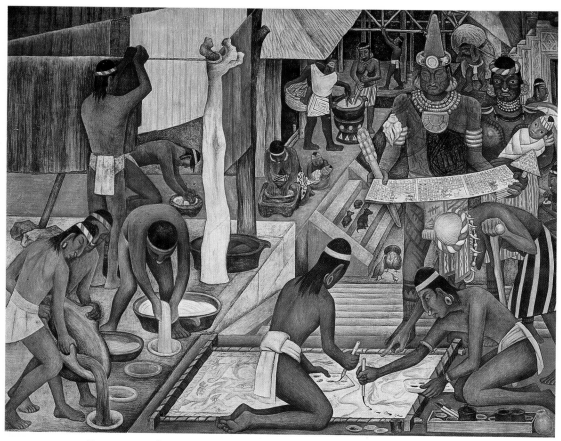

Tarascan Civilization (1942), fresco, Mexico City National Palace mural.

Peasants (1947), oil on canvas.

The Ice Breakers (1956), oil on canvas.

(continued from page 48)

Paris was difficult, especially with a newborn infant to care for. Fuel and milk could scarcely be found. Yet it was impossible to return home. Mexico was in ruins; bandits and rebels controlled the countryside.

The couple sent their son to live with a family in the suburbs, where he could receive better care. Rivera was now a major figure among the so-called classical cubists, advocates of a scientific approach to art. He read science books and joined weekly discussion meetings at the home of the prominent French artist Henri Matisse. There he met the revolutionary Russian writer Ilya Ehrenburg and a lesser known Russian artist, Marevna Vorobiev-Stebelska.

Six years younger than Rivera, Vorobiev was the daughter of a Russian official and a Jewish actress, opposite in every way to Beloff. In contrast to Beloff's gentle attractiveness, Vorobiev possessed a wild sort of beauty. Like Rivera, she was bad tempered and even violent. Rivera found Vorobiev "terribly exciting" and left Beloff to live with Vorobiev. After only six months, however, Rivera ran back to Beloff, claiming that life with Vorobiev "sapped his energies."

In the spring of 1917, Rivera's predictions came true. Half the French army mutinied, the British and French urged U.S. president Woodrow Wilson to join them in defeating the Germans, and the U.S. Congress declared war and urged young men to volunteer. One million men were needed. In the first 6 weeks, though, fewer than 100,000 joined the U.S. armed forces. Congress had to legislate a draft.

German troops had also invaded Russia, and thousands were killed each week in the bloodbath there too. Tired of hunger and war, Russian soldiers and their families at home demanded peace negotiations. Their anger finally propelled them to revolution.

In the early hours of October 25, 1917, a Russian named Leon Trotsky led thousands of workers in a successful insurrection, taking over the capital. Dressed in rags, the revolutionaries crowded into a fashionable school that night to hear Lenin, the most famous of the Russian revolutionaries, tell them, "We shall now proceed to construct the socialist order!" He promised to give land to the peasants, put the workers in charge of industry, and end Russian participation in the war.

Trotsky called on all the participants in the war to negotiate peace, but the Allied leaders wanted total victory so that they could dictate the terms of an armistice. They spread lies that Lenin and Trotsky were German spies. On March 3, 1918, Trotsky signed a separate peace with Germany.

With the addition of fresh young men from the United States the tide finally turned against the Germans. On November 11, 1918, Germany signed an armistice agreement.

The socialist revolution in Russia had an enormous impact on Rivera. He and his Russian émigré friends became enthused about returning to the new Soviet Union and helping develop a new people's art and literature. Rivera and Modigliani applied for visas but were turned down.

The whole issue of people's art caused Rivera to question cubism. If working people were to learn to control their own lives and run their own farms and factories, then they must learn the truths of history. Art could play an important role in the education of workers, but to do so it had to be accessible, not hidden away in museums and galleries but painted on the walls of public buildings. And it would have to deal with subject matter that could be understood. It should be used as a tool to help working people know their own history, their own worth as the real creators of the wealth of their nations.

Rivera began to believe that Picasso's outstanding work was for the wealthy, that it would never reach the masses. "He lacks a genuine universality," he commented later. "It would be hard to imagine Picasso's canvases hanging in any kind of worker's home." He reexamined the works of Pierre-Auguste Renoir and the Dutch masters of the 17th century, lush and revealing scenes of people talking, laughing, eating, filled with humanity and sensual feeling.

Renoir's own butcher and woodman had bought his paintings. Rivera's old friend the engraver Posada had told him to paint what he knew and felt. Perhaps that was Mexico. In Europe he was still a visitor, an exile.

With the war winding down and the curfew lifted, the cafés of Paris were once again filled night after night till the early morning. But when Rivera went to see Rosenberg or any of his old friends they considered him a traitor to art with his new ideas. He fell ill with vague liver and kidney problems and once again prescribed radical diets for himself.

Rivera turned to new friends who agreed with him. One was the physician and art historian Élie Faure. Rivera met Faure in uniform on the day of demobilization and painted him. It was one of the first of his many noncubist psychological portraits. Faure took Rivera to see an operation in a French hospital, and years later Rivera used the experience to paint *A Surgical Operation* in his fresco at the Ministry of Education in Mexico City. Faure agreed with Rivera that the artist had to relate to the events around him. Later he sponsored a group exhibit that included Rivera's new noncubist work.

In the fall of 1918, Rivera's two-year-old son was returned home. With so much of Rivera's art income now cut off, his home was cold and food was scarce. Little Diego fell ill and died before the year ended. Rivera and Beloff buried him and moved away from Montparnasse. Rivera's notorious affair with Vorobiev had crushed Beloff, and the death of their son was a final blow. Rivera now thought more often of Mexico.

Rivera's early 1919 meeting with an aspiring 21-year-old artist named David Alfaro Siqueiros only confirmed his longing to paint something new and revolutionary in Mexico. Siqueiros had fought with Obregón's forces against Villa, rising to the rank of captain. He had seen up close the Mexican Revolution's bloodshed—2 million dead. Now he was a functionary in Mexico's Paris consulate.

In Rivera's studio, Siqueiros observed beautiful line drawings of French peasant women harvesting grapes. For more than a

Rivera painted the mural Feast of the Day of the Dead *for the Ministry of Education building in Mexico City. In this panel from the mural, Rivera painted himself, hat tilted to one side, peering out of the crowd of celebrants.*

year, Rivera and Beloff all but shared their apartment with Siqueiros. While Beloff slaved away on her reproductions to pay the rent and buy food, the two Mexicans talked long into the night about art and revolution. Rivera listened spellbound to Siqueiros's stories of the Mexican Revolution.

But all was not well in Mexico. On April 10, 1919, the widely admired peasant revolutionary leader Zapata was lured into a trap by President Venustiano Carranza's representatives and assassinated. What no army could accomplish, an assassin's bullet did. Killing Zapata ended the Morelos Commune, taking the wind out of Mexico's revolutionary sails. Rivera and Siqueiros decided that a truly Mexican art must be created to help advance the Revolution's original goals of land for the landless, workers' rights, genuine popular democracy, and national ownership of natural resources.

In 1920, Mexico's ambassador to France, Alberto Pani, paid Rivera handsomely for portraits of himself and his wife and urged

Rivera to spend time in Italy studying Renaissance art. In February, Rivera left for a 17-month stay in Italy to examine the frescoes of the old masters. He traveled throughout the country, sometimes sitting for days sketching in front of an old masterwork. In the Sistine Chapel in Rome, he stayed for weeks, analyzing and drawing Michelangelo's famous frescoes on the ceiling. The chapel's nine enormous panels told the story of the book of Genesis in the Bible. The frescoes had been there since their completion in 1512—more than four centuries ago. That was the kind of work Rivera wanted to do.

Meanwhile, Mexico's political wars were heating up. Carranza was assassinated on May 21, 1920. Obregón was elected president in September, but the United States refused to recognize his government until 1923, when he agreed to protect foreign oil interests. Rivera believed that with Obregón as president, a revolutionary artist would now be able to work in Mexico. He began making preparations to leave for home. He helped produce a ringing manifesto, the end product of his discussions with Siqueiros two years earlier.

Calls to the Plastic Artists of America was first printed in Paris in May 1921. Written by Siqueiros as a summary of "the results of my exchange of ideas with Rivera," it called for a free public mural art "for the people" instead of expensive gallery art "for the individual." It urged a new synthesis in art that would merge the best of the new European art with the masterworks of the "lost" Indian civilizations of Mexico.

In June 1921, Rivera said good-bye to Beloff, promising her that he would send for her as soon as he was resettled and had enough money. Beloff commented many years after they parted, "Though he loved me for a few years and then other women, his painting was all he ever truly and deeply loved." Rivera never denied that he was difficult and perhaps impossible to live with. Of Beloff he said, "She gave me everything a good woman can give to a man. In return, she received from me all the heartache and misery that a man can inflict upon a woman."

Rivera's Girl with Mask, *which he painted in 1939, is another example of the artist's more sensitive pieces. Though not as overtly political as the artist's murals, these smaller pieces depicting Mexican peasant life are nonetheless imbued with Rivera's relentless social conscience.*

CHAPTER FIVE

Years of Glory

Rivera was ending his long apprenticeship. "On my arrival in Mexico," he wrote, "I was struck by the inexpressible beauty of that rich and severe, wretched and exuberant land." Once given the chance, he would express that "inexpressible beauty" in all its tragic yet hopeful splendor.

Minister of Education José Vasconcelos, an energetic patron of Mexican art, invited Rivera on a trip to the southern Yucatán Peninsula. There, on November 26, 1921, a sea of bright red Communist banners greeted them. Rivera saw how the administration of Governor Felipe Carrillo Puerto forgave the debts of the poor and distributed land to the peasants. When counterrevolutionaries executed Carrillo Puerto in January 1924, Rivera immortalized him in his murals at the Ministry of Public Education and, later, at the National Palace.

While he was in the Yucatán, Rivera camped out at the Mayan ruins of Chichén Itzá. He gazed spellbound at the 12th-century frescoes of the Temple of the Tigers. Here was the source of inspiration he had sought for so many years.

Rivera's enthusiasm electrified Vasconcelos. The minister immediately asked him to do a mural at the Preparatoria, as the National Preparatory School was called, and later at the new Ministry of Public Education building.

By the end of 1922, Rivera completed *Creation*, a magnificent, 1,000-square-foot mural at the Prepatoria. As he finished it, however, Rivera was disappointed, believing it was an imitation of European painting from the Byzantines and Italians through Cézanne. He was determined to create art that was distinctly and consistently Mexican.

In December, he welcomed Vasconcelos's offer of money to travel to the Isthmus of Tehuantepec, one of Mexico's most picturesque areas. There, Rivera finally left the Europe an influences behind. The Amazonian size and dignity of Tehuantepec's Indian women impressed him. They still looked and dressed as they had in ancient times, when they had ruled over a matriarchal society. He drew hundreds of sketches in his *Tehuantepec Notebook*— a veritable gold mine of line drawings he would use in murals throughout his life.

All of Rivera's subsequent murals portrayed Indians favorably and their oppressors negatively. In his National Palace mural, he depicted the Spanish conquistador Hernán Cortés as a syphilitic hunchback and the Aztec leader Cuauhtémoc as a youthful hero. At the Palace of Cortés in Cuernavaca, he painted an anonymous Indian dressed in a jaguar costume plunging a knife into the heart of a Spanish knight in armor.

Invariably, Rivera's murals looked to a brighter future: scenes like the one of young and old people sitting in a circle around a teacher at a literacy class in an open field or the ones of workers arming themselves and the poor emerging triumphant (Ministry of Education frescoes). Thus, Rivera set out to celebrate not the government of the Mexican Revolution that provided him with walls but the struggling masses who fought the Revolution only to be betrayed.

For the next several years, Rivera worked up to 16 hours a day and completed hundreds of frescoes at several mural sites—more than all the other Mexican muralists combined. Most of the time he was involved in other art projects as well—easel painting, water-colors, mosaics, stained-glass windows, editing and drawing for magazines, woodcuts for peasant leagues, stage-set designs.

Meanwhile, back in Paris, Beloff waited in vain for word from her lover. She sent countless letters and cables appealing to Rivera to send for her, but Rivera sent her only small amounts of money. Then, in 1922, he married Guadalupe Marin.

Beloff lived alone for the rest of her life. In 1933, she came to Mexico and passed within a few feet of Rivera in a concert hall, but he showed no signs of recognizing her. Like most of the women in Rivera's life, Beloff bore him no ill will. "Given my life to live over again," she said, "I would still choose to live those ten years . . . over again with him."

Rivera became obsessed with his new wife. He considered Lupe, as he called her, the perfect feminine form, and her figure found its way into many of his murals and paintings. Lupe Marin was in many ways similar to Marevna Vorobiev. Rivera described her as "a strange and marvelous-looking creature, nearly six feet tall . . . black haired, yet her hair looked more like that of a chestnut mare than a woman's. Her green eyes were so transparent she seemed to be blind. Her face was an Indian's, the mouth with its full, powerful lips open, the corners dropping like those of a tiger. . . . She was round-shouldered, yet slim and strong and tapering."

Like Vorobiev, Marin had a quick temper. Rivera found her personality exciting, but as with Vorobiev, he later commented that "her jealousy and possessiveness gave our life together a wearying, hectic intensity." Marin was perfectly capable of physically attack-ing women who showered too much attention on her husband. She had little interest in art or politics and resented the long hours Rivera spent at work. Often there was a shortage of funds in the Rivera household. Rivera supported his low-paying mural work by

Rivera gives a rousing speech to Mexican workers during the 1920s. For a number of years a member of the Communist party, Rivera sometimes took his political beliefs to the streets, earning the nickname the Lenin of Mexico.

selling his paintings, watercolors, and drawings. His nonmural artwork won prizes and plaudits.

But the money was gone almost as soon as Rivera received it. Marin resented his donations to the Communist party, of which he was now an active member, his frequent handouts to homeless men and women, and every dollar he spent on his beloved pre-Colombian relics. Once she ground up a few of the statues, spread hot sauce on top of the mess, and served it for dinner. Since he had spent their food money on his idols, she roared, he could eat them.

Mexico became a mural mecca and Rivera was the master. Foreign artists traveled great distances to learn at his feet. At the Education Ministry's new building, several of Rivera's assistants painted their own murals—either there or in other locales later. They included Fernando Leal, Jean Charlot, Ramón Alva de la Canal, Amado de la Cueva, Xavier Guerrero, Carlos Merida, and for a year or two Siqueiros and Orozco.

Most of Rivera's fellow muralists esteemed his art while disliking his personality. But Orozco, nicknamed el Tigre (the tiger) because of his impulsiveness and moodiness, went so far as to dismiss Rivera's art as a "poor imitation" of the Indian works of ancient times.

Rivera could be equally harsh in his own judgments. Early on, he said Orozco "caters to a herd of bucking jackasses" and Siqueiros "feels restless and broods" because no one has "proclaimed his great merit." But when Rivera saw their 1924 murals at the Preparatoria he changed his tune. Of Orozco's *Revolutionary Trinity* he said, "Good painting and deep emotion, such beautiful work." He called *The Burial of a Worker* and *Monarchy and Democracy* by Siqueiros "the most complete synthesis of our race to be realized since pre-Cortesian times."

Credited with the reintroduction of fresco painting, Rivera at first experienced some serious problems finding the right media. One day, Charlot found him "crying and viciously picking off his day's job with a small trowel as a child will kick down a sand castle in a tantrum." The muralists hopped on buses to various outlying towns in a mad quest for advice from Mexico's masons and house painters. They learned much from them and from the Mexican people's ex-votos and pulquería paintings. As Charlot later wrote, "Money can buy no better color for fresco than the earth pigments sold in any *tlapalería* [hardware store]." Charlot, de la Canal, Revueltas, and Emilio García Cahero were actually the first to use the fresco technique—in June 1922. Rivera quite effectively fused the techniques of Mexican masons and tips from Charlot with the fresco methods he had learned in Europe.

While Rivera painted feverishly and solved his fresco problems, he also involved himself in other tasks, such as organizing a trade union of artists. Receiving about two dollars a day, Rivera took pride in being a worker, rather than a mere artist. The real union organizer, though, was Siqueiros. A common expression became "Diego painting, Siqueiros speaking." While Orozco and

Leal were only lukewarm to Siqueiros's idea of a trade union of free plastic workers, Rivera applauded it. Soon, Rivera and Siqueiros were working together to form the Union of Technical Workers, Painters, and Sculptors, which they eventually founded. The union's manifesto lambasted gallery art and championed art for the people, and its members committed themselves "to destroy all egocentrism, replacing it by disciplined group work."

From the outset, conservatives marshaled a nationwide campaign against the new mural movement. As early as July 22, 1922, Charlot wrote in his diary: "A student gangs up with four others to give me a beating." Rivera always packed a gun when on the scaffold. The first murals to be defaced were those by Leal and Charlot on the Preparatoria's main stairway.

There was no doubt that the motive for the 1923–24 campaign of mural vandalism was political. During June and July of 1923, Rivera completed six panels in the education building's Court of Labor. As Rivera's revolutionary proletarian message took shape on the walls, conservative journalists sharpened their knives. Mexico City's leading newspaper *Excelsior* called Rivera "the bad painter of ugly things." The press coined the term *feismo* to describe Rivera's "ugly monkeys" and applauded the student vandalism directed at the murals.

Vasconcelos quickly capitulated to the conservatives. In January 1924, he tendered his resignation. He was persuaded to stay on the job, but he no longer had any desire to back the muralists. Knowing this, the press stepped up its attacks.

Rivera complained: "The ocean of stupidity is swelling. . . . [Vasconcelos] wishes no more obnoxious paintings. Times grow troublesome. One after another the scaffolds disappear." Later, at the education building, he painted Vasconcelos astride a white elephant dipping his pen into a spittoon.

In June 1924, egged on by a rabid press and by their own teachers, students stoned and mutilated Orozco's and Siqueiros's recent murals at the Preparatoria. Rivera signed a union protest that blamed reactionary teachers as the true culprits behind the students' attacks. Vasconcelos dismissed Siqueiros and Orozco and then resigned. In August, a presidential decree suspended most other mural work.

Rivera resigned from the union in July 1924. Charlot later observed: "Rivera's chances of finding work with the incoming government [of president-elect Plutarco Elías Calles] were materially increased as he disentangled his fate from that of the sinking Union." Siqueiros concurred. As far as he was concerned, Rivera was an "opportunist," a man whose principles came second to his own personal gain.

Through all of the controversies and brickbats, Rivera continued to work on the Ministry of Education murals. He also painted some self-portraits on the walls, one of which showed a moody Rivera as an architect. Another had him looking somberly out from a crowd of revelers celebrating the Feast of the Day of the Dead.

In August 1924, Rivera painted the words *Pearls Before Swine* on the prow of a boat in one of his lower stairway murals at the ministry. This was his way of counterattacking those who vandalized art. In early 1925, more certain of government support, Rivera deleted the words.

Then, on September 4, 1924, one of Rivera's staircase murals was defaced. The Ministry of Education ordered the stairway closed to traffic while Rivera mended the work. Vasconcelos's successor, J. M. Puig Casauranc, praised Rivera as "the philosopher of the brush." The tide started to turn back in Rivera's favor.

Visitors who flocked to see Rivera's murals at the education building in downtown Mexico City were overwhelmed by their size and free-flowing rhythm, the glowing luminescent colors, and the sheer power of their composition and message. The murals incorporated, and seemed to become part of, the sunshine that knifed through the building's portals and windows. The art was a celebration of labor and revolution, of popular festivals and the arts, of folk ballads and science. It covered the stairways, ceilings, and walls of every side of the 3-story-high, 2-block-long building— 124 frescoes totaling 17,000 square feet.

Rivera started painting the education building in March 1923 and finished in November 1928, completing several other major murals along the way. Despite international acclaim, Rivera's dissatisfaction with his own work persisted.

Meanwhile, Lupe Marin nagged Rivera about his personal hygiene, in particular his tendency, when he was extremely absorbed in his work, to go for days without a bath. Nonetheless, in August 1924, Marin gave birth to their first daughter, Lupe, who resembled her mother and whom they nicknamed Pico (pointy head). Though happy about the baby's arrival, Rivera spent very little time with his family: He had walls to paint.

In November 1924, Rivera began work on the administration building at the agricultural school in Chapingo. In 30 frescoes, he depicted the distribution of land to peasants. Two facing panels contrasted bad government and good government, one showing a ruined coastal area attacked by tanks and battleships (reminiscent of the U.S. invasion of Veracruz in 1914 to protect foreign oil interests and arm the Carranza-Obregón forces then fighting Zapata and Villa); the good government panel showed a thriving harbor. The final panel showed peasants and workers coming together to build a better society.

In early 1925, Rivera ordered the destruction of the already defaced Guerrero panels, Charlot's *Dance of the Ribbons*, and de la Cueva's painting at the education building on the grounds that they were not compatible with the overall design of the building's other murals. In April, Rivera resigned from the Communist party to devote himself full-time to his art. Three months later, he returned to the party.

As always, Rivera worked on two and sometimes three murals simultaneously. In April 1926, he moved on to the chapel of the Chapingo school. There, he extended his portrayal of opposites and painted his ideal of the peasants' dream of the Mexican

This panel from Rivera's 1924 mural at the agricultural school in Chapingo depicts the distribution of land to the peasants. The mural consists of 30 panels and tells the story of land reform and the coming together of government, workers, and peasants to form a better society.

Revolution. He designed a carved wooden double door, depicting the poor people of Mexico facing the wealthy in their top hats and tuxedos. Once the door was opened, an amazing sight loomed on all sides. Every round window of the chapel and every panel of the ceiling and walls was covered with brightly colored paintings.

According to the artist, the Chapingo frescoes were "essentially a song of the land." Rivera's symbol for nature was a "colossal, dreaming woman." His model for nature was Lupe Marin. Pregnant with their second child, he used her to represent the fecund Earth and then again to depict Earth "enslaved by monopoly . . . a bound prisoner surrounded by three symbolic oppressors, Clericalism, Militarism, and Capitalism."

But another woman also posed for the nudes in Rivera's chapel murals. She was Tina Modotti, called a femme fatale by José Vasconcelos. Modotti had come to Mexico City from California with her lover, photographer Edward Weston, whose acclaimed nude photographs of her had made her famous. Rivera's brief fling with Modotti enraged Marin. But Modotti, who openly preached her belief in free love and rejected the idea of being faithful to one partner, was no long-term threat to Marin. For Modotti, Rivera was simply her lover for the moment, although they also became good friends.

In 1926, Rivera joined the Hands-Off Nicaragua Committee, an organization that sought to force the evacuation of U.S. troops from Nicaragua. A feisty young rebel named Augusto César Sandino and his army eventually defeated the U.S. Marines through prolonged guerrilla warfare (1926–33). Rivera was very active in the pro-Nicaragua campaign for years, becoming secretary-general of the Anti-Imperialist League of the Americas. Many Americans joined the movement. Their protests and Sandino's military victories forced the U.S. Congress to call for a troop withdrawal from Nicaragua. Rivera felt proud.

In 1927, Lupe Marin invited her younger sister from Guadalajara to visit her. When Marin came home one day to discover Rivera and her sister in bed together, she became enraged, threatened to shoot off his right arm, and destroyed several of his canvases. Then she packed and left with her sister for Guadalajara.

For a time, Rivera stopped painting and wandered the streets, eating and sleeping very little. Finally, he went to Guadalajara to persuade Lupe Marin to come home with him. Shortly after that, Rivera fell from a scaffold at the Chapingo chapel and landed unconscious on the floor.

For three months he stayed home in bed, recovering from a severe concussion. During that period, Marin gave birth to a second daughter, Ruth. Darker-skinned than her sister and bearing more of a resemblance to her father, Ruth was nicknamed Chapo, an Indian word reflecting her copper skin tones.

As soon as Rivera recovered, he went back to climbing the scaffolds at the education building. He painted the controversial Wall Street banquet panel, showing the billionaires John D. Rockefeller, Sr., J. P. Morgan, and Henry Ford dining on ticker tape. He also designed the sets and costumes for a Carlos Chavez ballet.

In September 1927, a friend from his years in Europe arranged a visit for Rivera to the Soviet Union to participate in the celebration of the 10th anniversary of the October Revolution as part of an official Mexican delegation. Living with Lupe Marin had become intolerable for Rivera. "I welcomed the invitation to the Soviet Union as a pretext to get away from her," he later admitted. Before Rivera left, the poet Jorge Cuesta told him that he was in love with Lupe Marin. Rivera gladly gave him "permission" to court her. Soon after Rivera left for the Soviet Union, Marin divorced him and married Cuesta.

In the Soviet Union for six months, Rivera loved the workers' marches and the celebration of athletes, scenes he sketched and later painted at Rockefeller Center. But he encountered difficulties as an art instructor at the stuffy Academy of Fine Arts. His advocacy of a people's art was resisted by both the social realist painters, who generally portrayed heroic, happy workers, and the avant-garde painters of abstract art. When Rivera started painting murals for the Red Army Club, his critics schemed against him, his assistants proved incompetent, and he eventually found himself in the hospital with a severe sinus infection.

Siqueiros wrote in his memoirs of a visit he and Rivera made to the Soviet ruler Joseph Stalin. According to Siqueiros, Rivera found Stalin's views on art narrow and left the meeting disgusted. Later, he painted an unflattering portrait of Stalin. In May 1928, the Soviet government asked Rivera to go home, claiming that he was needed there. Rivera left in a huff, but on June 14, 1928, he happily set foot on *tierra azteca*.

When Rivera married the Mexican painter Frida Kahlo in 1929, she was 22 years old—21 years his junior. Kahlo, the daughter of jewelry store workers—Guillermo Kahlo, a Jewish Hungarian immigrant, and Matilde Calderón, a Mexican—contracted a debilitating bone disease as a young girl and lived most of her life in great physical pain.

CHAPTER SIX

The Most Important Fact

When Rivera returned to Mexico from the Soviet Union, he plunged headlong into politics, directing the presidential campaign of Communist party candidate Pedro Rodríguez Triana, despite veiled threats from Calles's emissaries.

Early in 1929, his last important Communist party assignment was the defense of his friend Tina Modotti. She had been charged with involvement in the murder of her lover, Julio Antonio Mella, an exiled Cuban Communist student leader. Mella was gunned down as he walked with Modotti down a Mexico City street.

Rivera played detective with relish, visiting the morgue, attending police hearings, and speaking at protest meetings. Modotti was deported, but Rivera and his friends continued digging for clues until they obtained proof of her innocence. Agents of the Cuban dictator Gerardo Machado y Morales had assassinated Mella. Cuba was forced to withdraw its ambassador and the chief Mexican detective resigned. Five years after viewing Mella's corpse at the morgue, Rivera painted it in a panel of the New Workers School series in New York.

Despite Rivera's activities, some officials in the Mexican government recognized the advantages of allowing the most renowned muralist in the world to continue creating new wonders. After the Modotti matter was resolved, Rivera painted at the Ministry of Health and Welfare six magnificent female nudes. Each nude symbolized an ideal—purity, strength, knowledge, life, moderation, and health.

Meanwhile, Calles was setting up the Maximato, the continuation of his rule behind a succession of puppet presidents until 1934. In short order, Calles ended the 1926–29 Cristero revolt sponsored by the Catholic church; cultivated good relations with the United States; slashed the budget for social reform; and began a ruthless crackdown on left-wing dissent.

Under the circumstances, Communist party leaders frowned on Rivera's acceptance of a commission to paint a mural on the staircase of the National Palace, site of top government offices, including Calles's. While Rivera sketched for the National Palace walls, the Communist party called for an armed uprising against Calles's one-man rule. Rivera believed this would lead to a bloodbath. Party leaders called him an opportunist. The Mexican government outlawed the Communist party until 1935.

In the late spring of 1929, Rivera became director of the Academy of San Carlos. He tried to convert the institution into a revolutionary workshop. He encouraged students to form a union of workers in the arts. Foundry workers, glassblowers, engravers, and other wage workers were admitted on a special basis. Actual work on a project replaced written exams. A student's first few years involved working days at a factory and attending the academy at night. Rivera encouraged students to find their own forms of self-expression—no more copying from plaster casts.

Along with his responsibilities at the academy, Rivera began long hours of work on the National Palace stairway mural. This *History of Mexico* project, often interrupted, would take several years and would become the most complete story of a civilization ever painted. It included nasty portraits of Calles and his puppets, even while Calles was still in power. Rivera considered this mural the "finest thing I had ever done . . . the only plastic poem I know of which embodies the whole history of a people."

Again, he would work on two major murals at the same time. Dwight W. Morrow, U.S. ambassador to Mexico, asked Rivera to paint a wall of the Palace of Cortés in Cuernavaca, Morelos. The nine-panel mural was to be a U.S. gift to the state of Morelos. But, before going to Cuernavaca, there occurred what Rivera later called "the most important fact in my life." He met the artist Frida Kahlo.

Kahlo seemed to embody the qualities Rivera admired most in women. While she could be nurturing, like Beloff, she could also be wild and outrageous, like Marin. Rivera admired independence in women at a time when few had their own interests and careers.

Frida Kahlo, like Rivera, was not only precocious as a child but also rebellious, mischievous, and disobedient. She also suffered hardship. At the age of six, she was struck with polio. For most of her life, Kahlo wore long dresses that covered her withered leg. In 1922, when she was 15, Kahlo became one of a handful of girls admitted to the Preparatoria. She planned to embark on a career in medicine. Cliques dominated the school and Kahlo was popular with all of them, but her real group, a brainy and mischievous bunch, was called the Cachuchas. When mural painting began at their school, the artists up on the scaffolds became perfect targets for the Cachuchas's practical jokes. They set fire to the scaffolds, exploded firecrackers, and burst water balloons over the painters' heads.

Rivera was one of the group's favorite victims. Kahlo often hid in a doorway and yelled taunts in Rivera's direction. She would call out, "Watch out, Diego, Lupe's coming," when another model was posing.

Kahlo spent much of her free time with the charismatic leader of the Cachuchas, Alejandro Gómez Arias. Kahlo and the handsome Gómez became lovers in 1923, but the two began to have trouble during the summer of 1925. A scandal emerged after a woman employee of the Ministry of Education library seduced Kahlo. Although she told Gómez that she loved him, Kahlo neither denied the rumor or others that she had many boyfriends.

On September 17, 1925, a terrible accident changed the course of Kahlo's life forever. Kahlo and Gómez were traveling home on a wooden bus when an electric trolley car plowed into it, splintering it into pieces and running over many of its occupants before it stopped. A broken handrail pierced Kahlo's body from one side to the other. Her spinal column and pelvis were smashed; her collarbone, ribs, and right leg suffered multiple fractures. Kahlo survived, but excruciating pain remained her companion for life. There was no way that she could stand on her feet for hours and become a doctor as she had planned. Instead, she turned to painting.

Despite their differences, Alejandro Gómez stood by Kahlo during the ordeal but left to study in Europe several months after

Kahlo painted this self-portrait in 1940. The artist once said of Rivera, "I cannot speak of Diego as my husband, because that term, when applied to him, is an absurdity. He never has been, nor will he ever be, anybody's husband."

Communist standard-bearers lead a crowd of more than 50,000 in a May Day parade in Mexico City. Rivera and Kahlo had a stormy relationship with the Communist party: Rivera was expelled from the party in September 1929, and Kahlo resigned over Rivera's expulsion.

the accident. When he returned, he fell in love with another woman. Until Kahlo met Rivera, she tried hard to win Gómez back.

Kahlo's friends could not understand how she could go from the good-looking Gómez to a fat, ugly old man. Her mother agreed and was especially upset by Rivera's atheism. But Kahlo was in love with her "Frog Prince." After a whirlwind courtship, 43-year-old Rivera married 22-year-old Kahlo in Coyoacán's city hall.

The couple moved into a house on the elegant Paseo de la Reforma in Mexico City. Several people came to live with Rivera and Kahlo in the house, including Siqueiros and his wife, two other Communist party friends, and a live-in maid.

On September 10, 1929, the Communist party expelled Rivera for disobedience, denouncing his acceptance of the San Carlos directorship. Rivera countered that he had turned down an offer to be minister of fine arts because he would not work for the government but that San Carlos, like the National University, was an autonomous institution. Wanting a people's artist as their director, the art students had elected him.

In typical theatrical fashion, Rivera presided over his own expulsion, with Kahlo seated beside him. He made a guerrilla theater joke out of the party hearing by putting a clay pistol on the table and accusing himself of "collaborating with the petit bourgeois government of Mexico." He then declared himself expelled, picked up the pistol, and snapped it in two.

Kahlo resigned from the Communist party over Rivera's expulsion. Many of their friends dropped them. Their "boarders" moved out. Modotti, whom Rivera had so enthusiastically defended, wrote Edward Weston that the great muralist was a traitor.

In the fall of 1929, Rivera took ill from the combined pressures of overwork, political battles, and snubs from old friends. Kahlo nursed him back to health. She made friends with Lupe Marin and learned how to prepare Rivera's favorite dishes.

In December, Ambassador Morrow and his wife went to London and Rivera and Kahlo moved into the Morrow summer home in Cuernavaca, a beautiful town on the low slope of a mountain about 50 miles from Mexico City. Rivera worked on the Palace of Cortés murals and Kahlo painted at home. After the hectic pace in Mexico City, it was a honeymoon for the newlyweds. Rivera's gorgeous mural portrayed the history of Morelos, beginning with the

This panel from the Rivera mural at Mexico City's National Palace depicts Aztec civilization in the city of Tenochtitlán. In December 1929, Rivera and Kahlo left Mexico City to spend the winter in Cuernavaca, where Rivera began work on a mural at the Palace of Cortés.

Spanish conquest and ending with the peasant revolt led by his favorite mural figure, Zapata.

Kahlo wanted desperately to have a baby, but her first pregnancy had to be terminated. Doctors disagreed on whether her weakened pelvis would ever be able to stand the strain of childbearing. She grieved for months and painted nightmarish fantasies of splintered bodies and floating fetuses.

The conservative administration of the National School of Architecture and others had marshaled a campaign for Rivera's removal as director of the Academy of San Carlos almost from the day he had taken the assignment. On May 10, 1930, the government complied by firing him.

It was simply one more indication that the euphoria of the first years of the mural renaissance was gone. Siqueiros had become a full-time political activist and was jailed in 1930 after tumultuous May Day demonstrations. He was confined to house arrest in the village of Taxco for the next two years. Orozco had been in the United States painting and teaching since 1927. Rivera could never be sure when the ax would fall on him.

Back in 1924, Kahlo had written to her sweetheart Gómez about saving up to go to San Francisco, the place she called the "City of the World." Her childhood dream was about to come true.

*Kahlo and Rivera arrived in the United States for the first time in November
1930, but their reputations preceded them. The eccentric, rotund genius
Rivera, with his radical leftist politics and coarse peasant manners, and
Kahlo, in her colorful Tehuana dresses and costume jewelry, took the
American art world by storm.*

CHAPTER SEVEN

Portrait of America

As his art fetched ever higher prices from buyers, Rivera became a darling of the American art community. American art patrons rushed to bring him into their personal orbit—even the very billionaires and their high-society wives whom Rivera condemned and ridiculed in his murals. The rich found the artist's rough manners and shocking leftist social message titillating. The very fact that they embraced the Lenin of Mexico, as they nicknamed Rivera, supposedly proved their broad-mindedness.

America's art patrons began inviting Rivera to the United States as early as 1926, but it was not until 1930, when the right-wing climate in Mexico became extremely dangerous, that visiting the United States became something he seriously considered. Mexico's fascist Gold Shirts—an armed group of racists and Catholic extremists who beat up on liberals, leftists, and "Indian-lovers"—were running wild.

In 1929, Rivera had been invited to paint a mural at the San Francisco Stock Exchange. He decided to seize this chance to paint the industrial civilization of the "imperialist colossus of the North."

If the Communist parties of the world labeled him an opportunist, so be it. He at least would carry his proletarian message directly to the masses of the world's most industrialized nation at a time when they were forming soup lines to survive the Great Depression.

The American art world was in a flutter at the news of Rivera's visit. In 1929, the American Institute of Architects had named Rivera winner of the Fine Arts Gold Medal. In 1930, his works were featured in an exhibition of Mexican art at New York's Metropolitan Museum of Art. In November, while these works went on national tour, a Rivera retrospective exhibition opened at the California Palace of the Legion of Honor. Private buyers snatched up any Rivera artwork they could find. In July 1931, the Rockefellers' prestigious Museum of Modern Art offered Rivera a one-person exhibition. It was only the second time the museum provided the space for a one-person show (the first was Matisse).

For a while it looked as though Rivera might never set foot on U.S. soil. The State Department refused him a six-month resident visa on the flimsy grounds that his Communist ideas could contaminate the American mind. It took a few well-placed phone calls by a wealthy San Francisco art collector before Rivera would be permitted to enter the United States.

In the middle of November 1930, Rivera and Kahlo arrived in San Francisco. But trouble was brewing. Envious California artists resented the choice of a foreigner. "Rivera for Mexico City; San Francisco's best for San Francisco" became their cry. Under screamingly patriotic headlines, newspapers printed photographs of Rivera's anticapitalist murals at the Ministry of Education.

Before long, however, Rivera's boyish ways and powerful painting, buttressed by Kahlo's charm and grace, captivated America. Rivera was his usual yarn-spinning self—a social lion at the receptions of the rich, a regular guy with taxi drivers and construction workers.

Loving the limelight, Rivera tipped his hat to the Americans. He called their skyscrapers, steel bridges, and machine-packed factories "the greatest expressions of the plastic genius of this New World," comparing their grandeur to that created by "the ancient people of Yucatán." In 1930, after watching an American football game, Rivera told a reporter: "Your game of football is splendid, thrilling, beautiful . . . fine color and design."

For two months, Rivera and Kahlo explored San Francisco, comparing the mansions on Russian Hill with breadlines in the streets below. Then, from December 1930 to mid-February 1931, Rivera painted his *Allegory of California* on the 30-foot-high walls and ceiling of the stock exchange's Luncheon Club. His model for California's "representative woman" was Helen Wills Moody, the tennis champion. Years later, Kahlo told a friend that Rivera spent a lot of time sketching the great athlete, disappearing for days.

After the stock exchange mural was officially inaugurated on March 15, 1931, Rivera received seven other mural commission

Rivera puts the finishing touches on his 30-foot mural at the San Francisco Stock Exchange. The large figure of a woman, representing the state of California, holds in her hands individuals engaged in the state's diverse industries, businesses, and professions.

offers. The very newspapers that earlier denounced him now sang his praises.

Exhausted, Rivera rested at the Atherton home of the San Francisco socialite Rosalie Meyer (Mrs. Sigmund Stern). There, in April, he painted a pastoral fresco in the alcove of an outdoor dining area. Then he returned to San Francisco to paint *The Making of a Fresco* in the gallery of the California School of Fine Arts (today's San Francisco Art Institute). The 1,200-foot fresco depicted painters, sculptors, and architects at work on a building with scaffolding. As models, Rivera used sketches he had done of American acquaintances. He also painted a famous, almost comical rear view of himself at work on the scaffold. Because the Mexican government was pressuring him to finish the National Palace murals, he worked day and night, completing the work in about a month.

On June 8, 1931, Rivera flew to Mexico to resume work on the National Palace. Unhappy with a section done in his absence by assistants, he repainted it. Then, with money from his San Francisco visit, he began building studio houses for himself and Kahlo in the San Angel neighborhood of Mexico City.

While he was still in San Francisco, the director of the Detroit Institute of Arts had invited Rivera to exhibit his work and paint a mural there. In late January 1932, Rivera began preparing the walls at the Detroit museum. He and Kahlo moved into a hotel across the street on April 21. When they later discovered that Jews were not allowed to stay in the hotel, Rivera shouted: "But Frida and I have Jewish blood! We are going to have to leave!" The hotel instantly ended its anti-Semitic policy.

For the next two months, Rivera toured and sketched the Ford Motor Company's River Rouge plant in Dearborn, Michigan. In June, he started painting *Detroit Industry*—27 fresco panels of the museum's Garden Court. Edsel B. Ford, son of Henry Ford and president of Ford Motor Company and the Detroit Arts Commission, funded the project.

Rivera called his Detroit murals "the great saga of machine and steel." Considered by some to be the best painting he did in the

Museum archivists examine a set of drawings that Rivera did in preparation for his Detroit Industry *frescoes, which he painted for the Detroit Institute of Arts in 1932. When a local priest objected to some of the mural's images, Rivera feared it might be destroyed, but in the end it survived the controversy.*

United States, they remain the world's most acclaimed painted vision of technology and science. Universal in their scope, they retain Rivera's love of all things Mexican. A large group of machines in one panel appears in the form of an ancient sculpture of the Aztec goddess Coatlicue.

Although in the United States he was constantly reminded of the harsh reality of capitalism—many living in dire poverty while others accumulated great wealth at others' expense—Rivera and Kahlo participated in the hypocrisy of the rich with gusto.

Rivera was on a first-name basis with Edsel Ford and painted his portrait. Still, they enjoyed embarrassing their hosts. For instance, Rivera laughed when Kahlo asked the notorious anti-Semite Henry Ford, "Mr. Ford, are you Jewish?"

There were also many difficulties for the famous couple. In the summer and fall of 1932, Rivera undertook a grueling vegetarian diet that almost killed him. He lost 100 pounds because he was

This section of Rivera's Detroit Institute of Arts mural, Detroit Industry, *shows the production and manufacture of the 1938 Ford V-8 engine. Many automobile industry leaders objected to the mural's images, claiming Rivera had portrayed assembly-line work as mechanized and exploitative.*

unhealthy and depressed. Kahlo experienced another miscarriage in July. She expressed her hurt in several paintings of dramatic, hypnotizing scenes of birth, death, dreams, and nightmares.

Claiming concern for Kahlo's health, Rivera later wrote that he "forbade her to conceive again." Kahlo's friend Ella Wolfe, the wife of the writer Bertram Wolfe, recalled that "Diego was very cruel to Frida about having a child. She was dying to have a baby by him." Ella Wolfe criticized Rivera for not allowing Frida to stay in bed for several months in order to have a baby. But Rivera, in his own words, had a higher "biological function of producing paintings" and could not be bothered. "For me painting and life are one," he liked to say.

Kahlo returned to Mexico in October to care for her dying mother. Meanwhile, Rivera went on painting. He also became active in a national campaign to aid millions of Mexicans being forcibly deported back to Mexico at the urging of employers who needed someone to blame for the massive worker layoffs taking place.

On March 13, 1933, Rivera completed his Detroit murals, which also provoked a storm of condemnation from conservative circles. Rivera was delighted when Detroit's industrial workers mobilized to guard his murals. He called it "the beginning of the realization of my life's dream." Edsel Ford and the Rockefellers joined the promural camp.

The outcry that greeted the covering of Rivera's RCA murals in May 1933 was no less sonorous. Artists and workers picketed Rockefeller's home, yelling, "We want Rockefeller with a rope around his neck! Freedom in art! Reveal Rivera's murals!" The New Workers School in New York City invited Rivera to paint there.

Rivera, whose RCA mural had recently been destroyed, addresses a crowd of Columbia University students, workers, and faculty as part of a demonstration in support of Donald Henderson, an economics instructor and avowed Communist, who was fired for his political views.

Rivera demonstrates his technique for art students at the New Workers School in New York City in 1933. Despite his enormous talent, dedication, and amazing body of work, Rivera was frequently criticized in the United States, mostly because of his left-wing politics. He and Kahlo returned to Mexico in December of that year.

The school was directed by Rivera's friend Bertram Wolfe and run by the Communist Party Opposition, a group of anti-Stalinist Communists sometimes called Trotskyists. Leon Trotsky had fought against Stalin's betrayal of the principles that had inspired the Russian Revolution. After Lenin's death, Sir Joseph Stalin, as Rivera called him, had emerged victorious. In 1928 he had stripped Trotsky of his citizenship and banished him. Living in the French countryside in 1933, Trotsky began to contact sympathizers around the globe to organize the Fourth International.

Rivera publicly declared that he agreed with Trotsky's thesis of Stalinist betrayal. Stalin's belief in building socialism in one country could not possibly work in a world of profit-hungry, aggressive capitalist powers. As Trotsky said, only revolution on an international scale could rid the world of war, poverty, and oppression and make possible a democratic socialism. Later, Rivera painted Trotsky's portrait in the New York City headquarters of a pro-Trotsky group and in the redone RCA mural at Mexico's Palace of Fine Arts.

Still fuming at the Rockefellers, Rivera used what was left of the money they had paid him to paint the New Workers School murals. As he wrote in *Portrait of America*, "For the first time, I painted on a wall which belonged to the workers . . . they all helped in the work." The result was perhaps the most complete history of the United States ever painted. The 21 movable fresco panels celebrated Daniel Shays, Abraham Lincoln, John Brown, Emma Goldman, and scores of other fighters for freedom. One of the panels showed Stalin the Executioner behind larger portraits of Marx, Lenin, Engels, and Trotsky.

Meanwhile, Rivera had a brief affair with the American artist Louise Nevelson. Tired of Rivera's affairs and homesick for Mexico, Kahlo insisted on going home.

Rivera raises his fist defiantly during a 1936 anti-Fascist demonstration in Mexico City as Kahlo looks on. That year, the Republic of Spain was invaded by Francisco Franco, and many Mexicans, particularly workers and peasants, took to the streets to show their support for the Republican resistance.

CHAPTER EIGHT

Out of Favor

Rivera and Kahlo moved into their new San Angel home, two separate modernistic cubes joined by a bridge. To some it seemed to symbolize their already eroded relationship.

Home seemed bleak after the triumphs of the Mexican mural renaissance and the U.S. murals. Kahlo wrote to a friend, "Because he doesn't feel well he has not begun painting . . . he thinks that everything that is happening to him is my fault, because I made him come to Mexico."

When the RCA murals were destroyed in February 1934, Rivera's depression deepened. He turned to Kahlo's sister Cristina for comfort, and an affair quickly developed. Deeply wounded, Kahlo cut off her long tresses and stopped wearing her Tehuana dresses. She was hospitalized three times that year.

In June 1934, Rivera's spirit lifted when he obtained permission to start reproducing a smaller version of the RCA mural that fall at the Palace of Fine Arts. Again, happiest when overworked, he began the final stairway wall of the National Palace mural in November with unflattering portraits of Mexico's *Men of the Revolution*. Completing the wall in a year's time, he painted Mexico's presidents and leaders dividing up the nation's wealth among themselves. He depicted Karl Marx pointing to a socialist future of peace and plenty.

Cristina Kahlo was at his side, posing and chatting as Rivera worked on the mural. Frida Kahlo moved to her own apartment in early 1935. She hoped that Rivera's fling with her sister would last only a short time, but Rivera set Cristina Kahlo up in a fashionable apartment and bought her furniture. Only as an afterthought did he buy furniture for his wife's flat. It was the first of many separations.

All of Frida Kahlo's friends urged her to break permanently with Rivera and to start by earning a living for herself as a painter. In July, Kahlo left for New York City, but her love for Rivera would not disappear. On July 23, 1935, she wrote her husband an unusual letter that dismissed all their affairs as mere flirtations. "At bottom you and I love each other dearly . . . we will always love each other." By that time, Rivera was tired of Cristina Kahlo and regretted hurting his wife. When he asked Frida to return to him, she quickly complied.

Life appeared to return to normal. Rivera painted in his studio and Kahlo in hers. Their home was again a hectic gathering place for visitors. Kahlo generously forgave her sister and attended dances, circuses, and street theater performances, once again in her lively Indian costumes. But appearances belied the truth. Kahlo drank heavily, and her paintings revealed her unabated rage. Kahlo told a friend that she felt as though she had been murdered by life.

On a daily basis, Kahlo took care of Rivera, mothered him, and indulged his every wish while he provided the money. He continued to chase women, but now Kahlo retaliated with her own affairs with both women and men. Unlike Rivera, who made no effort to hide his affairs, Kahlo was very discreet. Still, gossip got the best of Rivera, who could not bear to hear his enemies talk about his cheating wife.

And Rivera was surrounded by enemies. The Communist party called him a painter of palaces for Yankee tourists. Siqueiros, the party's spokesperson in the art world, regularly denounced Rivera as a "saboteur of the collective work." On August 26, 1935, Rivera and Siqueiros spoke at a conference on education at the Palace of Fine Arts. A vehement debate between the two muralists concluded with the two middle-aged artists facing off with pistols in hand, each denouncing the other's art and politics.

When President Lázaro Cárdenas surprised everyone by not acting like another Calles puppet, the Left rallied to his cause. Cárdenas ejected Calles from Mexico in April 1936, enacted land and labor reforms, and nationalized the oil industry in 1938. The Communist party became ardently pro-Cárdenas, and consequently there were no new government walls for Rivera, an open Trotskyist. For the rest of his life, Rivera received fewer government commissions than Orozco or even Siqueiros (whom the government nonetheless expelled in 1941).

Rather than try to ingratiate the Cárdenas administration, Rivera, with his customary rebellious flare, made matters worse by officially joining the Trotskyist International Communist League in September 1936. But he fell ill and was hospitalized twice in 1936 with eye and kidney infections.

Willing to paint, even for next to nothing, Rivera went to work that summer on his *Carnival of Mexican Life* mural at the new Hotel Reforma for a mere $1,000. Its owner was Alberto Pani, the man who had helped him get to Italy in 1920, now one of Mexico's many "revolutionary" millionaires. The Reforma was a gathering place for American tourists, but Rivera seemed to go out of his way to insult his old friend's customers, painting into the mural grotesque images calculated to offend the Americans.

Pani paid Rivera and called in his two architect brothers to rub out the insulting images. Rivera responded by confronting Pani at the mural site, armed with two pistols. Rivera was thrown in jail for the night. But upon his release, he won a suit to restore his work. Later, it was sold to his dealer, Alberto Misrachi.

In the middle of these artistic battles, both Rivera and Kahlo remained politically active. On July 18, 1936, the Republic of Spain was invaded by a Fascist general, Francisco Franco. Few people realized it then, but World War II was on the horizon. Both Adolf Hitler and Benito Mussolini used the Spanish civil war as their military testing ground for upcoming invasions of Europe. Rivera and Kahlo, with other supporters of Spanish democracy, formed a committee to raise money for the Loyalists, the supporters of the Republic. In a few weeks, they both were embroiled in a far less popular and more dangerous action involving Leon Trotsky.

Trotsky was living in Norway when he was tried in absentia at the so-called Moscow Trials in 1936. Accused of treason and terrorism, he and other leaders of the Russian Revolution were found guilty. Trotsky was sentenced to death. The Norwegian government refused to send Trotsky back to the Soviet Union but asked him to leave. With no other government willing to risk inviting him in, Trotsky was a man without a country.

Toward the end of November, Rivera received a cable from friends in New York urging him to attempt to help Trotsky settle in Mexico. To Rivera's surprise, Cárdenas, tired of gossip that he was under the total control of the Communist party, offered Trotsky political asylum if he steered clear of Mexican politics.

On January 9, 1937, an oil tanker docked at Tampico, Mexico, and Leon and Natalia Trotsky disembarked. They were whisked away to Kahlo's blue house in Coyoacán, where they lived rent-free for the next two years under heavy guard.

Trotsky organized an international commission to examine the evidence presented at the Moscow Trials. John Dewey, the American educator and philosopher, served as chairman. The first session was held on April 10, 1937. Rivera and Kahlo attended. The Dewey Commission found Trotsky innocent and strongly condemned the Stalinist Soviet regime.

Rivera and Kahlo socialized with the Trotskys. They made a disparate foursome: Leon and Natalia Trotsky, formally dressed and behaving conservatively; Rivera and Kahlo, known for their wild garb and outrageous behavior.

Frida Kahlo escorts the exiled Russian revolutionary Leon Trotsky and his wife, Natalia, from their ship onto Mexican soil in 1937. The Trotskys lived with Kahlo and Rivera for the next two years in Coyoacán and then moved into their own house

Perhaps in continued retaliation for Rivera's affair with her sister, or perhaps charmed by the courtly European mannerisms of the famous Trotsky, Kahlo quickly seduced the revolutionary leader. First they slipped notes to each other and then began having secret trysts in Cristina Kahlo's house. Everyone in Trotsky's political party, including his wife of 35 years, seemed to know about the affair, while Rivera either did not see what was going on or pretended not to.

Trotsky's followers were concerned that the Stalinists would use the affair to sully Trotsky's reputation. On July 7, they took the Old Man, as they called him, to a farm about 80 miles away from Mexico City. Frida Kahlo visited him there a few days later. Shortly after the visit, Trotsky returned to Coyoacán and his depressed wife, reassuring her of his love at the same time that he wrote a nine-page letter to Kahlo begging her not to break off with him. Frida Kahlo sent the letter to a woman friend. "I am very tired of the Old Man," she wrote.

On November 7, 1937, the 20th anniversary of the Russian Revolution and Trotsky's birthday, Kahlo presented Trotsky with a flattering and sensual self-portrait.

When art circles began to notice her paintings during the late 1930s, Kahlo went to New York City to prepare for an exhibit. The New Year arrived, and Kahlo moved on to Paris for another exhibit. She hated the French capital, finding the cafés oppressive. "There is something so false and unreal about them that they drive me nuts."

With Frida Kahlo gone, Rivera still spent time with the Trotskys, but there were frequent political arguments. The outbreak of World War II was the final straw. Trotsky said it was only one more war between capitalist countries. Rivera thought that fascism had to be fought even if one had to unite with capitalists. Trotsky tried to undermine Rivera's influence in the Mexican Trotskyist group. On January 11, 1939, Rivera resigned from Trotsky's Fourth International. In April, Trotsky moved to another house in Coyoacán. He left behind Frida Kahlo's self-portrait.

Kahlo and Rivera filed for a divorce in the fall of 1939 and refused to make statements to the press. Some thought that Kahlo, now earning her own living, no longer had to put up with Rivera's skirt-chasing ways. Others insisted that the cause was the American movie star Paulette Goddard, who was living across the street from Rivera while he painted her portrait.

Rivera and Kahlo remained friends. On several occasions, Rivera appeared in the concert hall of the Palace of Fine Arts with his daughters, a current mistress, Cristina Kahlo or Lupe Marin, and of course, a spectacularly bedecked Kahlo.

Although in public Kahlo appeared to be her usual devilish, happy self, the reality was different. A month after the divorce she abandoned her usual way of dress and took to wearing mannish suits. Again suffering excruciating spinal pain, she was encased in one terrible body cast after another. By the end of 1939, she consumed a full bottle of brandy every day.

Rivera's portrait of American film actress Paulette Goddard. When Rivera and Kahlo filed for divorce in 1939, many suspected that one reason for the breakup was Rivera's infatuation with Goddard, who lived across the street from them at the time and occasionally modeled for him.

As the conflict between Stalin and Trotsky continued, Rivera apparently wanted to make it plain that despite his break with Trotsky, he had little love for Stalin. In 1940 he wrote an article for *Esquire* magazine in which he called Joseph Stalin the undertaker of the Russian Revolution.

On May 24, 1940, Siqueiros, dressed in a military uniform and riding on horseback, led a group of armed men to Trotsky's well-guarded compound in Coyacoán. The Trotskys hid under their beds as their rooms were sprayed by bullets. Siqueiros was tried and jailed until Cardenás exiled him a year later. He went to Chile to paint murals.

Before Siqueiros's arrest, Rivera, because of his well-known conflict with Trotsky, was among the suspects. Invited to paint a mural in San Francisco, he left Mexico. From June 1940 until February 1941, Rivera worked on his movable Treasure Island mural. Its theme was "Marriage of the Artistic Expression of the North and South on This Continent," and it was his largest work to date. It reflected Rivera's internationalist beliefs through the use of Indian, Mexican, and Eskimo representations, as well as images from the United States. After 20 years in storage, it found a home in the lobby of the Arts Auditorium of San Francisco City College. In one corner of the mural, Rivera and Paulette Goddard appeared holding hands. "American girlhood . . . shown in friendly contact with a Mexican man" was how Rivera described his intent. Behind them stood Frida Kahlo, alone.

Kahlo was indeed alone, in Mexico, and her physical condition worsened. She became friendly with a member of Trotsky's entourage who called himself Jacques Mornard but whose real name was Ramon Mercador. On August 20, 1940, Mercador, who had ingratiated himself in the Trotsky household through his relationship with an American secretary working there, entered Trotsky's study and savagely struck him from behind with a mountaineer's ice pick. Stalin's orders had been obeyed: Leon Trotsky lay dead.

Kahlo telephoned Rivera in San Francisco and told him of Trotsky's murder. Because of her friendship with Mercador, she was dragged down to police headquarters and questioned for 12 hours while other officers ransacked Rivera's studio. Fearing he might be blamed for Trotsky's death, Rivera hired bodyguards to watch over him on his scaffold.

Warned by a friend that their separation could prove harmful to Kahlo's health, Rivera sent for his wife. She arrived in early September and checked into a hospital. Rivera brought a guest with him when he came to visit—the public relations officer for the Golden Gate International Exposition, Heinz Berggruen. "You are going to be very much taken by Frida," Rivera told him.

Just weeks later, Kahlo traveled secretly to New York with Berggruen. They stayed for two months at the Barbizon Plaza hotel,

Rivera and Kahlo apply for a marriage license in San Francisco on December 5, 1940. They remarried three days later, on Rivera's 54th birthday. Around this time, Kahlo's health began to deteriorate rapidly, and she became increasingly dependent on Rivera for financial and emotional support.

attending parties and seeing the sights. Rivera called frequently with ardent marriage proposals and finally Kahlo accepted on the condition that they have no sexual relations with one another and that their finances remain separate. "I'm going to marry her because she really needs me," Rivera told friends.

On December 8, 1940, Rivera's 54th birthday, he married Kahlo for the second time. They stayed together for two weeks and then Kahlo went home for Christmas.

In February 1941, close to 100,000 people crossed the Bay Bridge to Treasure Island, where they viewed the unveiling of Rivera's completed mural. Now that his work was done, it was time to go home. Siqueiros had been captured, and Rivera was no longer under suspicion. This time the couple lived in the blue house in Coyoacán, with Rivera using the San Angel residence as his studio.

Rivera painted Women with Flowers *in 1943. That year, with the Mexican government and the Communist party united in the war against Nazi Germany, the Mexican government's attitude toward the Left improved. Rivera was appointed to the Colegio Nacional and was offered a position teaching composition and painting at the National School of Painting and Sculpture.*

CHAPTER NINE

God Is Dead

On June 22, 1941, the Nazis invaded the Soviet Union. As the Russian people fought to save their homeland, Rivera started to revise his opinion of Stalin the Executioner and applied for readmission to the Communist party. But the party leadership was leery of having the unpredictable artist back in its fold and rejected his application. For the next 14 years, Rivera made repeated attempts to gain readmission to the party. He denounced certain of his past political positions and exploits and even went so far as to express disdain for the politics of some of his paintings. He supported every twist in the party's "correct line."

By 1943, the Mexican government and the Communist party were united in their war against Germany. The government attitude toward Mexico's left-wing artists improved, and Rivera was appointed, along with Orozco, to the prestigious Colegio Nacional. Rivera taught composition and painting at the National School of Painting and Sculpture. Kahlo taught there as well until, unable to commute, she instead invited young artists to come to the blue house.

Four students, ranging in age from 14 to 19, came there regularly for several years. Rivera and Kahlo obtained walls for them at local bars and hotels. The Fridos, as they called themselves, often painted controversial murals. Kahlo and Rivera helped them find jobs and arrange shows of their own.

Rivera now received government commissions. The first, at the Institute of Cardiology, was a two-wall fresco on the theme of religion versus science. By his standards, it was a mediocre depiction of great persons in the history of medicine. The second was to return to the National Palace and paint its corridor. Working off and on for several years, he painted panels idealizing earlier civilizations. His depiction of the Aztec capital of Tenochtitlán remains a bright spectacle of color, detail, and cultural splendor.

Rivera had always dreamed of being a multitalented "Renaissance man," in the tradition of the Italian artist Leonardo da Vinci. During the war years, he started constructing Anahuacalli, a three-level pyramid-museum-studio in the rocky Pedregal district near Coyoacán, to house his pre-Colombian art treasures. By the end of his life, the structure housed 60,000 pieces, Mexico's largest private collection.

Kahlo joined Rivera in this expensive project, worrying about finding the money to complete it. At first the joint venture helped her to keep him close, but not for long. They separated again in 1944. "Diego is not anybody's husband and never will be," she told a friend, "but he is a great comrade."

In the spring of 1946, Kahlo submitted to spinal surgery in New York City, but the operation only worsened her condition. She developed a chronic inflammation of her bone marrow. While Kahlo was hospitalized in New York, Emma Hurtado replaced Misrachi as Rivera's art dealer. Before long, much to Kahlo's dismay, Hurtado was in love with Rivera and running the household.

In 1947, Rivera became a member of the Commission of Mural Painting at the National Institute of Fine Arts. He was joined by Orozco and Siqueiros (who had returned to Mexico in 1944 after his 1941 expulsion). Thus, the Big Three at last were together—as

Rivera painted this portrait of the gallery owner and art dealer Emma Hurtado in 1946. As Kahlo's health deteriorated, Rivera became romantically involved with Hurtado, whom he married in 1955, a year after Kahlo's death.

part of the government they so despised. But, according to Siqueiros, they quarreled more than ever.

That same year, Rivera started work on *Dream of a Sunday Afternoon in the Alameda* for the Hotel del Prado, a work he completed in 1948. In the foreground of this poetic and playful mural, considered among his very best, Rivera painted himself as a chubby little boy, a mischievous expression on his face, holding the hand of a *calavera* (skeleton for the Day of the Dead). The skeleton's other hand rests on the arm of the master of all calavera artists, Rivera's early inspiration, Posada. Behind this magical trio, a maternal-looking Frida Kahlo holds a small sphere of life's conflicting principles, the yin and the yang. Nearby stand Rivera's two daughters, dressed as elegant ladies. In another section, Rivera painted next to Juárez a figure of an anticlerical Liberal hero holding up a scroll with the words *God does not exist.*

Catholic students raided the hotel, scratched out the atheistic scroll, and gashed the image of Rivera as a boy. Mobs stoned Rivera's San Angel studio. Rivera refused to eliminate the scroll, and his mural was covered. In 1956, Rivera called a press conference at the mural site. Cameras flashed as he slowly painted out the atheistic slogan and announced, "I am a Catholic." He explained that he admired the Virgin of Guadalupe, "the standard of Zapata." His maiden aunts, who had prayed so many times for Rivera's salvation, had not lived to see this day. The mural was publicly shown at last.

In August 1949, a 50-year retrospective of more than 1,000 Rivera art works opened at the Palace of Fine Arts. The ultraconservative Mexican president Miguel Alemán Valdés referred to Rivera as a national treasure. On September 7, 1949, Orozco died and was accorded high honors as well. A year later, Rivera received the National Art Prize.

But a fresh scandal excited the press and public more than government appreciation of Rivera's great art. Rivera was in love with a glamorous Mexican movie star, María Felix, and was about to divorce Kahlo and marry the actress. Though the rumor was not entirely true, Rivera, flattered by the idea that such a glamorous woman would find him attractive, did not deny it. Kahlo moved out. Then, when Felix refused to marry Rivera, he returned to Kahlo. "Frida was happy to have me back," he claimed.

But Kahlo seemed anything but happy. Her paintings during that period were weeping self-portraits. By early 1950, her right leg was severely infected, and even huge doses of painkilling drugs were no longer adequate to control her misery. Hospitalized for a year, she submitted to a spinal operation, bone grafts, and painful experiments—all to no avail. Rivera often stayed overnight at the hospital in a small room next to hers. In 1951, Kahlo went home in a wheelchair.

But Rivera did not curtail his artistic or political activities. With Siqueiros he campaigned for an international meeting—the Stockholm Peace Convention—to protest the atomic bomb. Alone, he attempted another innovation—painting murals underwater. The Lerma Waterworks murals deteriorated within a few years, but outside the Lerma pumping station he did an immense and striking mosaic. That same year he planned a mosaic relief of the history of sport for the National University stadium.

As he approached his 67th year, Rivera remained extremely active. In the spring of 1952, the National Institute of Fine Arts commissioned him to paint a mural-sized work for a European tour of Mexican art. In 35 days, Rivera completed *The Nightmare of War and the Dream of Peace,* a powerful statement in which Stalin and Mao Zedong, the Communist leader of the Chinese Revolution, are shown inviting leaders of the United States, Britain, and France to sign the Stockholm Peace Petition. Rivera painted Uncle Sam with a machine gun on his back, a Bible in one hand and a fistful of dollars in the other, standing in front of a black man nailed to a cross. The director of the institute refused to exhibit the work, and the government also cut off funding for his stadium mosaic.

In April 1953, it was obvious that Kahlo, now a frail invalid, would not last much longer. Friends organized her first one-person exhibit in Mexico. Since she was unable to leave her bed, they moved the bed to the gallery. There, decked out in her Tehuena finery, she greeted those who came to honor her. In August, doctors agreed that it was going to be necessary to amputate Kahlo's right leg. Privately Rivera said, "This is going to kill her."

After the surgery, Kahlo refused to return home until Hurtado left the blue house. Unable to cope with Kahlo's suffering, Rivera plunged feverishly into his work and what would be his last fresco commission. He expanded his Institute of Cardiology theme of 1943 in the Hospital de la Raza of Mexico's Institute for Social Security. Rivera called the work *The People's Demand for Better Health*.

Spring briefly lifted Kahlo's spirits. Unable to sit upright, she tied herself to the wheelchair and painted a little. She talked of her upcoming wedding anniversary on August 21, and made plans for travel and future work. July 2, 1954, was the last time Kahlo was seen in public. She left her bed and with Rivera pushing her wheelchair joined 10,000 others in a march to protest the U.S.-sponsored invasion of Guatemala. The U.S. Central Intelligence Agency (CIA) had launched an effort to overthrow a democratically elected president and install a regime that would protect the interests of the United Fruit Company. Kahlo's right hand was clenched in a fist as she rolled down the avenue for four hours shouting with Rivera, "*Gringos asesinos, fuera!*—Yankee assassins, get out!"

When she returned home, Kahlo developed pneumonia. Somehow she knew it was the end. On July 13, she gave Rivera a ring, his anniversary present, in advance. He stayed by her bedside until she was sound asleep and then left for his studio. During the night, Kahlo died.

Rivera went with Hurtado and Lupe Marin to the blue house. The two women dressed Kahlo in her favorite Tehuena outfit and braided her hair with flowers. Rivera stayed in his room, refusing to see anyone. Frida Kahlo's coffin was left open for viewing at the Palace of Fine Arts. The director had granted permission to use the premises if there would be no banners or demonstrations.

Even at this sad moment, Rivera provoked an incident. Frida Kahlo undoubtedly would have enjoyed it. Suddenly the flowers were removed from Kahlo's casket and the Communist flag appeared—huge, red, a hammer and sickle across it. Honor guards watched over the coffin as 15,000 people walked by to view Kahlo's body. The last watch included Siqueiros, ex-President Cárdenas, and his son Cuauhtémoc Cárdenas. In his autobiography, Rivera wrote, "July 13, 1954, was the most tragic day of my life. I had lost my beloved Frida, forever."

In July 1957, Rivera opened the Coyoacán house to the public as the Frida Kahlo Museum. One of Kahlo's last paintings, a still life of watermelons, still hangs there. Painted in red above her signature is the phrase VIVA LA VIDA—LONG LIVE LIFE.

On September 25, 1954, Mexico's Communist party finally readmitted Rivera. His first painting after that was a scathing denunciation of the U.S. intervention in Guatemala. The work immediately went on a tour of the Soviet bloc countries.

Toward the end of June 1955, Rivera married Emma Hurtado. On August 24, 1955, they traveled to the Soviet Union at the invitation of the Moscow Fine Arts Academy. In the fall, he checked into a Moscow hospital for symptoms that to this day remain a mystery. His stay was brief, and in 1956, Rivera toured the socialist countries of Eastern Europe. He then returned to Mexico for the winter months. On December 8, 1956, Rivera celebrated his 70th birthday. The government declared it a day of national homage.

Rivera sketches in front of Moscow's Cathedral of St. Basil. During the mid-1950s, Rivera visited the Soviet Union, where he received treatment for what some believe was a cancer condition. While there, he told an interviewer, "I love Moscow and I love the Soviet Union. If I have to die of cancer I should die here."

Though Rivera's health declined, he continued to paint and sketch, looking forward to major new murals. But in September 1957, a blood clot paralyzed his right arm. On November 24, 1957, sometime after midnight, he died of heart failure.

Rivera received official honors at the Palace of Fine Arts. Among the guards of honor were Siqueiros and former president Cárdenas. Thousands viewed his body and marched in his funeral procession. There was, of course, a disturbance at his funeral ceremony when Communist party militants unfurled their red flags, but Siqueiros calmed the crowd. Rivera was buried at the Rotunda of Illustrious Men at the Pantheon of Dolores, Mexico City.

An enormous crowd of mourners gathers to join Rivera's funeral procession through Mexico City two days after his death on November 24, 1957. Rivera's body was laid to rest at the city's Rotunda of Illustrious Men at the Pantheon of Dolores.

Diego Rivera, one of the great artistic geniuses of the 20th century, was a man of passion, conviction, and vision. He loved life, lived it to its fullest, and left behind a stunning body of work that to this day stands as a moving tribute to the decency of common people.

Rivera left behind not only a wealth of great painting but the very idea of a people's art, inspiring others to paint with a social conscience. Some years after Rivera's death, a new people's art emerged in the United States, one that influenced artists on both sides of the Mexico-U.S. border and around the world. Inspired by the movement for civil rights and an end to the Vietnam War during the 1960s, artists in black, Latino, and Asian communities as well as in white ethnic neighborhoods painted thousands of murals. Most of the money to fund the projects was donated by local merchants and families. Even today, murals and other creative work reflecting the spirit and dignity of working people adorn the walls of our cities.

In the decades since Rivera's death, Rivera's legacy has endured, and it is likely to endure for some time to come. For wherever there is greed, exploitation, and oppression, Rivera's defiant spirit will be at work against these forces.

Chronology

1886   Born Diego María Rivera in Guanajuato, Mexico, on December 8

1892   Moves to Mexico City

1896   Begins taking art classes at Academy of San Carlos

1903   Joins anti-Díaz strike and is expelled from the academy

1907   Arrives in Spain on subsidy from Veracruz governor

1909   Falls in love with Russian artist Angeline Beloff, in Paris

1910   Mexican Revolution begins; leaders such as Pancho Villa, Álvaro Obregón, and Emiliano Zapata step forward to lead the charge against the Díaz regime; Rivera designs a poster urging Mexican peasants to support the revolution

1911   Returns to Paris and moves in with Beloff

1913   *Girl with Artichokes* marks Rivera's experimentation with cubism

1914   World War I begins; Rivera and Beloff move to Spain

1916	Beloff gives birth to Rivera's first child; Rivera leaves Beloff for an affair with another Russian artist, Marevna Vorobiev-Stebelska; returns to Beloff six months later
1919	Rivera meets Siqueiros; birth of daughter María
1920	Zapata killed by an assassin's bullet; the revolution in Mexico falters; Rivera goes to Italy to study Renaissance art; Obregón elected president after the assassination of Venustiano Carranza
1921	Rivera leaves Paris for Mexico; Beloff stays behind
1922	Starts Preparatoria mural; joins artist union and Communist party; marries Guadalupe Marin
1923	Starts Ministry of Public Education murals
1924–28	Completes murals at Ministry of Public Education and Cipango; breaks with Marin, who in turn marries poet Jorge Cuesta; becomes active in the Hands-Off Nicaragua Committee and becomes secretary-general of the Anti-Imperialist League of the Americas; visits the Soviet Union
1928–29	Completes murals at Ministry of Health and Welfare, National Palace, and Palace of Cortés; appointed director of the Academy of San Carlos; marries Frida Kahlo; expelled from Communist party for accepting directorship of the academy
1930	Fired from directorship of the academy; Rivera and Kahlo visit California
1933–35	Controversy over the RCA Building mural results in its destruction; RCA mural redone at the Palace of

Fine Arts; Rivera has brief affair with American
artist Louise Nevelson

1936–40   Joins the Trotskyist International Communist
               League; Russian revolutionary Leon Trotsky and
               his wife live with Rivera and Kahlo in Mexico for
               several years; Kahlo and Rivera divorce; Trotsky
               is assassinated; Rivera and Kahlo remarry

1942   Rivera starts building Anahuacalli

1946   Kahlo undergoes spinal surgery; Emma Hurtado
               becomes Rivera's art dealer

1949   Fifty-year retrospective held at the Palace of Fine
               Arts in Mexico

1950   Rivera wins National Art Prize

1952   Completes *The Nightmare of War and the Dream
               of Peace*

1954   Kahlo dies; Rivera readmitted to the Communist
               party

1955   Marries Emma Hurtado; hospitalized in the
               Soviet Union

1957   Dies of heart failure on November 24

Further Reading

Arquin, Florence. *Diego Rivera: The Shaping of an Artist, 1889–1921.* Norman: University of Oklahoma Press, 1971.

Brenner, Leah. *An Artist Grows Up in Mexico.* Albuquerque: University of New Mexico Press, 1987.

Charlot, Jean. *The Mexican Mural Renaissance 1920–1925.* New Haven: Yale University Press, 1963.

Cockcroft, James D. *Mexico.* Rev. ed. New York: Monthly Review Press, 1990.

Founders Society, Detroit Institute of Arts. *Diego Rivera: A Retrospective.* New York: Norton, 1986.

Garza, Hedda. *Leon Trotsky.* New York: Chelsea House, 1986.

Gleiter, Jan, and Kathleen Thompson. *Diego Rivera.* Milwaukee: Raintree, 1989.

Haney, John. *Vladimir Lenin.* New York: Chelsea House, 1988.

Hargrove, Jim. *Diego Rivera: Mexican Muralist.* Chicago: Childrens Press, 1990.

Herrera, Hayden. *Frida: A Biography of Frida Kahlo.* New York: HarperCollins, 1983.

Hurlbut, Laurance P. *The Mexican Muralists in the United States.* Albuquerque: University of New Mexico Press, 1989.

Katz, Friedrich. *The Secret War in Mexico: Europe, the United States, and the Mexican Revolution.* Chicago: University of Chicago Press, 1981.

McMeckin, Dorothy. *Diego Rivera: Science and Creativity in the Detroit Murals.* East Lansing: Michigan State University Press, 1985.

O'Connor, Francis V., ed. *The New Deal Art Projects: An Anthology of Memoirs.* Washington, DC: Smithsonian Institution Press, 1972.

Ospovat, L. *Diego Rivera.* New York: Progress (USSR), 1989.

Parkes, H. B. *A History of Mexico.* Boston: Houghton Mifflin, 1969.

Ragan, John David. *Emiliano Zapata.* New York: Chelsea House, 1989.

Rivera, Diego. *My Art, My Life.* New York: The Citadel Press, 1960.

———. *Portrait of America.* New York: Covici, Friede, 1934.

Wepman, Dennis. *Hernán Cortés.* New York: Chelsea House, 1986.

———. *Benito Juaréz.* New York: Chelsea House, 1986.

Wolfe, Bertram D. *The Fabulous Life of Diego Rivera.* New York: Stein and Day, 1963.

Index

JAMES COCKCROFT holds a Ph.D. from Stanford University. A three-time Fulbright scholar and a visiting professor at the State University of New York at Albany, he is a consulting editor for this series. He has written several books on Mexico and Latin America, including *Daniel Ortega* for the Chelsea House series WORLD LEADERS—PAST & PRESENT, and he is co-author of *Toward a People's Art.*

RODOLFO CARDONA is professor of Spanish and comparative literature at Boston University. A renowned scholar, he has written many works of criticism, including *Ramón, a Study of Gómez de la Serna and His Works* and *Visión del esperpento: Teoría y práctica del esperpento en Valle-Inclán.* Born in San José, Costa Rica, he earned his B.A. and M.A. from Louisiana State University and received a Ph.D. from the University of Washington. He has taught at Case Western Reserve University, the University of Pittsburgh, the University of Texas at Austin, the University of New Mexico, and Harvard University.